S0-CNE-116

# Under
# the Texas Sun

A · WARDLAW · BOOK

# Under
# the Texas Sun

ADVENTURES OF A TEXAS COWPUNCHER

## Anna Manns Dana

TEXAS A&M
UNIVERSITY PRESS
COLLEGE STATION

Copyright © 1986 by Anna Manns Dana
All rights reserved
Manufactured in the United States of America
First Edition

Chapter opening drawings are adapted, by permission
of the artist, from the illustration for chapter 14
of *The Wonderful Country,* by Tom Lea.

*Library of Congress Cataloging-in-Publication Data*

Dana, Anna Manns.
  Under the Texas sun.

  (A Wardlaw book)
    1. Vernon, Malcolm Graham, 1861–1936.   2. Cowboys—
Texas—Biography.   3. Ranch life—Texas—History.
4. Texas—Social life and customs.   I. Title.
II. Series.
F391.V47D36   1987      976.4'06'0924   [B]      86-14401
ISBN 0-89096-284-7

# Contents

# Contents

# Preface

My grandfather, Malcolm Graham Vernon, was a storyteller, and he must have been a spellbinder, for whenever any two members of his family or friends got together, at some point one would say, "Remember Papa's story about . . . ?" Only a few weeks before he died in 1936 did his children realize that these wonderful tales would be lost if they were not set down. The children would sit by his sickbed encouraging him to tell the stories of his youth and days as an early Texas cowboy, riding the range under the Texas sun. But his time to reminisce ran out, and not enough of his stories were preserved.

My mother kept family history records, letters written before and during the Civil War, and letters from her father to his mother written in the 1880s. My aunt saved the diaries my grandfather kept all his life; the earliest is a leather-bound one he carried on roundups and cattle drives. My uncle wrote down the stories he remembered of his father's life on the Half Circle Six Ranch; it was his intention to write this book. To me, the eldest grandchild, fell the lot to inherit the family records, the letters, the diaries, and my uncle's notes—and the duty to record them.

I am grateful to my grandparents' three children, Rhea J. Vernon, Kate Vernon Manns, and Rose Vernon Johnson. Without my uncle's unfinished stories, rough drafts, and outlines,

I could not have recalled the stories; had I not heard my mother and aunt retell the stories, I could not have understood his notes. I have three regrets: When I could have heard the stories firsthand, I was too young to be interested. I waited too long to write them down; all the people who could have helped recall them have died. I did not know my grandfather's exact words. Much of the fascination of any tale is in the telling, and he was the master storyteller.

The early family history was drawn from handwritten records, some made four generations back, and from *The Garlington Family* by T. K. Scogland. The names of the nonfamily characters are either the names recorded by my uncle or fictional. In writing the stories I admit to some fiction and frills, but not so much as to change the facts as they were given to me.

My brother, Malcolm Rhea Manns, and my cousin, Malcolm Vernon Balmer, are the family genealogists and have been of invaluable help. To them, the Malcolms of the last two generations, I dedicate this book.

# Publisher's Acknowledgment

The Texas A&M University Press is privileged to add its imprint to this Wardlaw Book. The designation claims a special place in the list of Texas A&M publications.

Supported with funds inspired by the initiative of Chester Kerr, former head of Yale University Press, this book, along with its companion volumes, perpetuates the association of Frank H. Wardlaw's name with a select group of titles appropriate to his reputation as man of letters, distinguished publisher, and founder of three university presses.

Donors of these funds represent a wide cross-section of Frank Wardlaw's admirers, including colleagues from scholarly presses throughout the country as well as those from other callings who recognize and applaud the many contributions that he has made to scholarship, literature, and publishing in his four decades of active service.

The Texas A&M University Press acknowledges with profound appreciation these donors.

Mr. Herbert S. Bailey, Jr.  
Mr. Robert Barnes  
Mr. W. Walker Cowen  
Mr. Robert S. Davis  
Mr. John Ervin, Jr.  

Mr. William D. Fitch  
Mr. August Frugé  
Mr. David H. Gilbert  
Mr. Kenneth Johnson  
Mr. Chester Kerr

*Publisher's Acknowledgment*

Mr. Robert T. King
Mr. Carl C. Krueger, Jr.
Mr. John H. Kyle
John and Sara Lindsey
Mrs. S. M. McAshan, Jr.
Mr. Kenneth E. Montague
Mr. Edward J. Mosher
Mrs. Florence Rosengren

Mr. Jack Schulman
Mr. C. B. Smith
Mr. Richard A. Smith
Mr. Stanley Sommers
Dr. Frank E. Vandiver
Ms. Maud E. Wilcox
Mr. John Williams

Their bounty has assured that Wardlaw Books will be a special source of instruction and entertainment to the reading public for many years to come.

PART ONE

# The Family

# Grandpa

My mother named me Malcolm. I was the ninth generation of her line to bear that name. There had been Malcolms in that family since 1660 when a daughter of Sir Malcolm Hatfield married James Dial of Scotland. As a child hearing of my legacy, I imagined them all as fierce as my grandfather.

Grandpa, Isaac Malcolm Dial, was born in South Carolina in 1808. When he was seventeen, he was sent to live with his grandmother in Tennessee. This move was meant to be a reprimand for his participation in an escapade involving a mock initiation of a slave named Uncle Abe Madden. The slave had said that he wanted to be a Mason. So the young boys in the neighborhood took him down to the river one midnight, built a fire, branded him with the Masonic symbol, and told him he was a Mason. When the incident was reported, Grandpa was packed off to Tennessee in disfavor, in disgrace, and beyond the wrath and reach of the owner of the slave.

In Tennessee he lived with his grandmother, attended school, read law, enjoyed his new independence, and married Grandma —something that further infuriated his father. His father felt that Grandpa was there as punishment and he just wasn't being repentant enough. In a fit of temper he disowned his eldest son and namesake.

Grandpa's family was great on disowning. In fact, he came

from a long line of disowners. His grandmother Honoria Garlington Coker had been disowned for eloping with William
Coker in 1780. It wasn't just the elopement that upset her father so much as the shame of her camping out overnight with
her fiancé and two friends on their way to the county seat for
the license and ceremony. To make matters worse, the young
people were set upon by some Indians and robbed of their
possessions, mostly their clothes. The next morning they entered town near-naked and were seen by her father's friend
before they could seek help. All this was just more than the
father could bear. He disowned his daughter and never al-
lowed her or any of her descendants to enter his home. His
will was filed in 1808 and makes no mention of his daughter,
who by this time was a widow living with her son and his family in Tennessee. It was to this family that Grandpa was sent
to repent and mend his wild ways.

Now it was Grandpa's fortune to be disowned and disin-
herited. He received nothing from his father, but his children
did.* This schism between Grandpa and his father had other
causes than just the initiation prank. The final break came with
their disagreement over Grandpa's choice of a wife. The Dial
family and the Patton family had once lived in the same part
of northern South Carolina. The Dials were for several generations considered the wealthiest in the district; the Pattons were
a pioneer family of modest means and eventually moved on
to Tennessee. Whether it was a feud between families, politics,
or just snobbery, great-grandfather Dial violently objected to
his son's marriage to a Patton.

---

*There is a probate record filed in Cherokee County, Tex., 1851, which petitions
that Isaac Malcolm Dial, Jr. (Grandpa), be appointed guardian for his minor children. It further states that his children had inherited considerable property willed
to them by their paternal grandfather, Isaac Malcolm Dial, Sr., of Laurens County,
S.C. All this was part of a seven-year court battle between Grandpa and his brother
in South Carolina, who tried to withhold all monies, property, and slaves for his own
use until Grandpa's children came of age. Grandpa won the suit, but by then the
lengthy litigation and the settlement had dissipated the inheritance.

The Pattons were Scotch—a proud, Protestant, Presbyterian family descended from Matthew Patton, "The Martyr." This Matthew was beheaded in Glasgow Square and his son, John, imprisoned because they were disciples of John Calvin and John Knox. John Patton was sent to America to serve a ten-year sentence in a prison colony in the Carolinas. Few of these prisoners survived the hardships of their internment, but John did. He returned to Scotland and in 1705 moved with his family to Pennsylvania.

John had a son, Matthew, born on the boat to America, and two grandsons, both named Matthew, born in Pennsylvania. Our Matthew ancestor moved on to Carolina and settled in the Waxhaw District—the section that later became part of South Carolina. Matthew's son, Alexander Patton, was a schoolmate and friend of Andrew Jackson, and as young men they moved together to Tennessee, served together in the Tennessee Militia, and bought neighboring property in Davidson County. Another neighbor of the Pattons and the Jacksons was James Coker, uncle of my Grandpa Dial. Alexander Patton married Jane Starr (cousin to the wife of Davy Crockett), and their youngest daughter, Jane Starr Patton, was my grandmother, Grandma Dial.

Grandma was born in Tennessee in 1810, married Grandpa in 1829, had her first child in Tennessee, her second in Georgia and her third in South Carolina. The next six were born in Alabama and the two youngest in Texas.

In Alabama, she and Grandpa owned a plantation on Elk Creek where it enters Muscle Shoals. Grandpa managed the plantation and practiced law. He had his office in his peach orchard. Their first home was built near the creek, but after the deaths of their five youngest children they abandoned that home and built another house on the upper end of the plantation in Limestone County, Alabama. When their baby girl, born in 1848, contracted the same illness that had caused the deaths of their other children, Grandma begged to move from the area. She was convinced that the clouds of vapor rising from the creeks flowing into the Tennessee River was the cause of their tragedies. This last child to have "the vapor sickness" (polio) survived but was crippled.

Grandpa traveled alone on horseback to Texas and selected a home and property in Cherokee County. In 1851 he moved his family, six slaves, and livestock to a farm near Rusk, Texas. Grandpa's eldest son, Garlington Coker Dial (my uncle Garley), nineteen, stayed in Alabama to complete his medical training. Two daughters, Nancy Amanda and Harriet, were eighteen and fifteen. Martha, still recuperating from her bout with polio, was two when they moved across three states by horse and wagon.

Nancy Amanda, called Nan, had helped her father in his law practice since she could read. For several years she had kept the farm records and the household and business accounts. She read law and wanted to be a lawyer. Her mother felt that this interest was unfeminine, almost shameful, and when family or friends came to call, Nan's books were hidden and the matter hushed up.

After the move to Texas, Grandpa gave up his law practice and became a full-time farmer. Grandma had two more babies: Sam, born in 1852, and Thomas in 1854. Harriet lived at home and helped with the younger children and Nan became a schoolteacher. From September to June she boarded with the minister's family in New Danville and taught at the one-room school near the general store owned by Thomas Vernon.

The Vernon family had moved to Texas in 1850 and bought a small farm near New Danville. Mr. Vernon was listed in the 1860 census: "Merchant living in Rusk County, Texas." The Vernon children attended the school where Nan taught. Callie, the oldest girl, was a self-appointed teacher's assistant and would often stay after school to help and visit with her new teacher.

One Friday afternoon Callie stayed to help with the weekly

sweeping and cleaning of the schoolhouse. Nan asked about her mother and the younger children at home. Callie confided that her mother was lonely for adult companionship and extended an invitation to come to see them. Nan missed her friends and family, and so the next afternoon walked out to pay a call on Callie and her mother.

Martha Chisum Vernon was a few years older than Nan. She had married young and had six children when she and Nan met in 1856. She worked hard caring for a family and managing a home and farm where the Vernons raised the food they ate and feed for their livestock. Though her husband did early chores and milked the cows before leaving to spend twelve hours at the store, most of the responsibility was Martha's. Her nearest relatives were in Tennessee, and since coming to Texas she had been too busy and tied down to make new friends. She was delighted to know this young teacher who had the time and the freedom to come visiting. The women formed an instant and close friendship.

For the rest of that school year and the next, it became routine for Nan to spend Saturdays at the Vernon farm. Martha's husband would take the buggy to town on Saturday morning, Nan would drive it back out to spend the day with Martha, then in the evening the trip would be reversed. The visits were filled with cooking, sewing, gossip, and shared confidences. By the fall of 1857 Martha was expecting her seventh child; she and Nan worked on the new layette together. The baby was due in February and Martha was counting on Nan's help and support.

In the middle of December Nan went home for the holidays. This was an exciting time at the Dial house, for there were lots of relatives around. Besides her parents, brothers, and sisters, there were aunts, uncles, and cousins. There were Hendersons, Colemans, two families of Davenports, and six other families of Dials. Of the thirteen children of the South Carolina Dials, eleven had moved to East Texas. So many people were always at Grandpa's that you couldn't tell who was living there, visiting, or just taking a shortcut through the house.

The first Saturday of the new year, Grandpa packed Nan, her clothes, and new gifts into the wagon. She returned to New Danville, arriving at the boardinghouse about midafternoon. She was putting her things away when there was a knock on the door.

It was Callie. Her face was swollen and she was out of breath from running. Nan knew that something was wrong and kneeled down to hold her even before she spoke.

"Oh, Miss Dial, Mama is gone. They buried her yesterday and they buried our new baby with her." They held each other and cried together.

Nan returned to the farm with Callie and the other children, who had been at the store with their father. They fixed supper and talked about Martha and how they would somehow manage without her. Callie, this little girl just nine years old, would have to take over all the responsibilities that had been her mother's. John and Miles, ages eight and seven, would help her, but they resented directives from women. Jim, Dee, and Robert were bewildered and confused by the changes and new routine, such as it was.

Propriety was necessary if Nan was to live in this small crossroads community and keep her job as the teacher. It would be thought shocking if she spent too much time at the Widower Vernon's home, so she and Callie planned and worked out problems at school. Four-year-old Dee was enrolled in the first grade, and the nearly three-year-old Robert was at the school as much as he was at the store, often napping on a pallet by the big wood stove. Nan arrived earlier to open the schoolhouse so the Vernon children could ride in with their father when he opened his store by seven A.M. Each Monday morning Nan watched anxiously for their wagon to pull up so she could see that the family had managed another weekend and all was well.

The school term ended in May, and Grandpa came to take Nan home for the summer. She and her father rode out to tell the children good-bye. This was her first time in several months to walk into the house where she had spent such happy times with her friend. After she left, she cried as much for Martha as for her family.

A month had passed when a peddler stopped by with a letter. It was from Callie. She wrote that Jim, Dee, and Robert had had measles but were recovered. Miles had cut his hand chopping wood, and John was limping after their milk cow kicked him. Dee had been lost several hours before they found her down by the creek. The only good news came at the end of the letter:

"Pa is so glad only three had measles that he says we should celebrate. He needs supplies from Henderson and he says we can ride over with him and stop by to see you. We will come sometime next week. Please be home for *I have something to ask you*."

When Thomas Vernon came to the farm with his brood and proposed, right in front of the children, she accepted—all seven of them. She adored these children; they already seemed hers, and she realized that at some point she had begun to love their gentle father.

My parents, Nan and Thomas Vernon, were married July 19, 1858. Nan's sister, Harriet, was hired to replace her as teacher, and the Saturday visits between the Vernon family and the New Danville schoolmarm resumed.

My brother, Thomas Rusk Vernon, was born in 1859. I was was born March 10, 1861—just one month after the attack on Fort Sumter.

2

# Papa

My father enlisted in Lane's Regiment, 1st Texas Rangers, and served with the Confederate forces in Arkansas and Louisiana. I do not have a clear recollection of him; he was just one of the men in the family, all serving alike in Confederate companies, coming and going on short furloughs. But I do remember sitting on a fence with my brothers watching for a team and wagon that was to bring him home from the war.

Papa had written Mama that he was ill with dysentery and asked her to send Grandpa, Miles, and a slave, called Negro Jim, to Louisiana, where he was in a hospital south of Alexandria. They put the bows on the wagon, fixed a bed of straw, and left to go for him and bring him home to convalesce. A week later when they hadn't yet returned, Mama posted her children down by the gate to watch the road for the first sight of them. It was another week before the returning wagon was sighted and we all shouted for Mama.

I can still see her dashing out of the house, handing my baby brother Albert to Callie, holding up her skirts, and running down the road to meet her husband coming home from the war. We jumped down from the fence and took off after her. I was the youngest and the last to catch up, and when I did I saw only Grandpa, Miles, and Negro Jim in the wagon. Mama was crying.

Papa had been much sicker than he had told her in his letter. The first night they camped beside the road, and he died while the others were sleeping. It was August, hot and humid, and they were a long way from home. Grandpa made the decision not to bring him home for burial but to bury him there in Rapides Parish, Louisiana. He told Mama that the grave was at the turn of the road under a large tree.

When my Grandfather Vernon died in 1871, a memorial stone was erected in the Old Vernon Cemetery near Toone, Tennessee. On the large limestone monument were engraved the names of Papa's parents, brother, and this inscription:

THOMAS GAINES VERNON
December 3, 1824–August 22, 1864
eldest son of
Nancy Epps Chisum and Robert Hicks Vernon

Papa died just three weeks before my brother Isaac Garlington Vernon was born. We called him Dick. He was born at our grandparents' home in Rusk and, at Grandma's insistence, we never returned to live at the farm near New Danville. Grandpa must have been a very forbearing fellow, for Mama moved home with ten children. For the next twelve years we lived with "the Family," and Grandpa ruled us all.

# 3

# Grapevine

Early in 1865 Grandpa moved his big family to North Texas—two hundred miles by wagon train. East Texas was good land for farming, but Grandpa and his eldest son wanted to raise cattle and go where there was open range land for grazing.

Uncle Garley had moved his family to Grapevine, Texas, before the war and before he went off to serve as a surgeon with the Confederate forces. He had advised Grandpa to move before the end of the war, which they both thought would be of short duration and with the South victorious. Grandpa would have made his move sooner, but Grandma refused to move so far away from my mother and her children until my father returned from the war. Now that was all changed. Grandpa decided that Mama would sell the store and her farm and move with the Family to a community near Grapevine called Lonesome Dove. No one ever questioned Grandpa's decisions, and I am sure that Mama did not want to be left behind.

Such a move was no small undertaking. There was property to dispose of, households to pack, and food to prepare for the long trip—for the stock as well as the family, which included Grandpa, Grandma, Aunt Harriet, Aunt Matt, my uncle Sam, Mama, and her ten children. Mama's children were Tommy, age six; myself, age four; Albert, age two; Dick, four months. This was the first of a two-part journey for my half-brothers and sisters: John, fifteen; Callie, sixteen; Miles, fourteen; Jim, thirteen; Dee, eleven; and Robert, ten. They were going to Tennessee to live with their grandparents.

I do not clearly remember my father's first family. We never saw them again, but Mama talked often of "her orphans," and she and Callie corresponded for over forty years. After Mama's death, I took over the letter writing and kept the link between us. That our family was to be divided was a difficult decision to be made, and Grandpa made it. Mama and their father had discussed the possibility of such an eventuality, and both sets of grandparents, who lived in the same community in southern Tennessee, had written wanting the children to come to them. Mama knew this was best for Martha's children. Later that year, after the roads were considered safer, they joined up with a wagon train coming through Dallas County and going to Nashville. With Callie and John in charge, they moved to Toone, Tennessee.

The move from East Texas was a hard move, I am sure, but to the children it was high adventure: the caravan of wagons, the men on horseback driving the livestock ahead of them, and the camping at night. None of the grown-ups wanted to make the change—except Grandpa—and least of all our slave Henry. Grandpa sold five of the six slaves he had brought with him from Alabama. Grandma refused to part with Henry, who was a favorite and a "member of the family." Henry moved with us.

We settled on the farm near Grapevine in the Lonesome Dove community. Uncle Garley's family lived in town. We all worked. Even the youngest learned to help with the cows, feed the pigs, tend the garden, work in the fields, hunt game, and pick wild grapes. Everyone seemed to adjust to the new home and life—except Henry. Henry was homesick for his friends and family. Grandma promised him that as soon as the spring planting was in, she would weave the material to make him a new suit, and he could go back to East Texas to visit his family. When the suit was finished, Grandpa wrote him a pass, necessary to prove that he was not a runaway slave, and Henry set out for home. As he walked out of sight down the road, Grandma turned to Grandpa and said, "Well, that's the last we will see of that suit." And it was.

A few days after Henry's departure, word came of Lee's surrender and we learned that the war was over. Grandma worried that something bad had happened to Henry, but Grandpa thought Henry just stayed in East Texas when he found that he had been freed. Anyhow, we never heard from Henry again.

By fall the family pattern was set. Uncle Garley was home from the war and was busy as the local doctor. Mama and Aunt Harriet taught school, Grandpa ran the farm, ruled the family, and organized a Masonic lodge. Grandma and her daughters kept us all clothed and fed. Our social and spiritual life centered on the Lonesome Dove Baptist Church. We were there often — all but Grandma. The Pattons had been Presbyterian since before they left Scotland in 1700, and Grandma wasn't about to change now.

No one had any money — certainly our Confederate money was worthless — but we had food on the table and a roof over our heads. These were hard times, but in later years I looked back on our North Texas days as secure and happy. To a child they were. My brothers and I attended a one-room school, where Mama taught, and had our chores before and after school. I liked working with the cattle best. I was no more than four when I would run ahead, open the gate for those half-wild cows to rush through, and then go in among them to help with the feeding. I could sit a horse as well as any man by the time I was eight.

Grandpa had been a Mason since his South Carolina days, and most of his social life and activity outside the farm was with the Masons. In 1868 the lodge members built the Grapevine Masonic Institute, which included the lodge and a schoolhouse. Grandpa was one of the members who took ox teams to the lumber mills in East Texas for the pine siding and helped fell the oak trees for the framing timbers.

The Monday in September that the new two-story schoolhouse was dedicated was an exciting day for all of us. There were speeches, a ribbon cutting, and dinner on the grounds. Mama and her sisters were laughing and visiting with their friends, Grandma was busy with the baskets of food, and Grandpa was running around being important. I remember playing among the wagons, yelling out the upstairs windows, and going to sleep in the wagon on the way home.

But these were the early years following the Civil War, and ours was the land of the defeated army. The adults did not find life as simple as did the children. Anxious and troubled days far outnumbered the happy ones. There were many homeless and hungry people roaming about the South. Discharged soldiers, both Union and Confederate, freed slaves, and opportunists lived off what they could beg, steal, or were big enough to take. This was the time of the carpetbagger, the Reconstruction governors sent down from the North, and federal troops who roamed the state. They took the saying "the spoils of war belong to the victors" in the broadest sense. North Texas was a stronghold for outlaws who had hideouts in the nearby Arbuckle Mountains of Oklahoma Territory—some notorious, others just plain lowdown horse thieves and renegades. All this led to the men around Grapevine banding together to form their own protection society. There was no listed membership, no elected leaders, just families helping others when there was a need. Different problems brought together different groups, and when the need arose they called themselves the "Ku Klux Klan."

Only once did I see the Ku Klux Klan in full robes.

Texas had a number of Reconstruction governors, each worse than the other until they hit bottom with E. J. Davis. Davis formed a state police of Negroes and scalawags. This band was accountable only to him, and they made life very difficult for the people of Texas. The night I saw the KKK form, they were preparing to make a raid into Fort Worth to call on some of Davis's state police.

About dusk Mama took us with her to sit with a neighbor. Grandma and my aunts were with us; in fact, all the women and children from the neighboring area were there, but no men. I was about ten then, and Albert was eight. We were old enough that Mama was not watching us all the time, and we went down near the barn to play with some other boys. One of the older boys told us the Klan was gathering that night and suggested that we slip off and watch them. He said they were meeting on his father's farm. We sprinted across a couple of fields and down a road and spotted them collecting in an open space surrounded by mesquite trees and low underbrush. We slipped up close and hid behind a bush. The horses were draped in white and all the riders were wearing long white robes and high white peaked hats. There was no talking. The only sounds were those made by the horses blowing and stamping their feet. Our hiding place was very near one rider who seemed to be the leader. He didn't give any spoken commands, just signals and gestures with his arms—lining up the riders and counting with his fingers, pointing occasionally. He was so busy organizing the group he did not notice that his horse kept shifting position, gradually moving in our direction. We did not notice this either for we were watching the Klansmen.

Suddenly the horse nuzzled his head right down at my brother's hand as if expecting a slice of apple or a lump of sugar. Albert was so startled that he blurted out, "Hey! That's Ole Buck!" and every Klansman there jerked his head in our direction.

The leader looked right down on us and I was looking up at him, eyeball to eyeball. He pulled on his reins, took a quick circle around that bush, and muttered in a low growl, "Get out of here, you little devils—NOW, GET FOR HOME."

We fell all over each other scrambling out of there, jumping over bushes, dodging cactus, sliding down ravines. We ran until we knew we were out of sight and then stopped to catch our breath.

We were resting beside the road, daring each other to go back, when we heard the sound of hoofbeats. We quickly rolled backward into the bar ditch, flattened out, and lay there watching as the white figures raced by single file. There was a long string of them, and Ole Buck was in the lead.

It was some minutes after the last horse was out of sight before any of us made a sound or a move. Then, without saying a word, we each took off in the direction of our own homes. Albert and I ran all the way home before we remembered that we were supposed to be at the neighbor's house. We made a dancing turn around, raced across the field, and were just going over the fence when we heard Mama calling for us, saying that it was time to go home.

Albert and I whispered and snickered all the way back to our house. We knew that Ole Buck was our horse and that someone with a voice *exactly* like Grandpa's was riding him.

The next day Grandpa was at the breakfast table and the conversation was as usual: "How was school yesterday, Mac? Albert, don't forget to repair that gate you swung on last week and broke. Mother, these peaches are the best we've had this year." Albert and I kept waiting for the axe to drop, but Grandpa never mentioned the night before and you can be sure that we didn't either.

We learned young to be closemouthed. We didn't talk about what we saw or heard, seldom among ourselves and certainly never outside the Family. The children knew most of what went on at home and in the community. We didn't always understand, but we were well aware of our precarious situation in those troubled times. I don't think my brothers and I were cowardly but, remembering back, it seems to me that we were often afraid. I can remember being afraid to sit out on the porch alone at night or go by myself to the privy after dark, afraid that a Republican or a Catholic or a carpetbagger would jump out, snatch me, and take me up north. The fear of Catholics came from Grandma's tales of her Scotch ancestors, and all my life I had heard of that terrible land north of the Mason-Dixon line, inhabited by Yankees, Republicans, and Feds—the enemy.

Much of our fear and anxiety came from the attitude of our womenfolk. The sound of a horse on the road, an unexplained noise, or the sight of a stranger in the area would make Mama or Grandma stop work, glance over a shoulder and look wide-eyed at each other. When the men were gone to their clandestine meetings, the women would talk in hushed tones, peer anxiously out the windows, and keep us close at home until the men returned. They never talked to us about their concerns, but we could sense their uneasiness and tension.

There were Indian raids occasionally, though our area never had one. Those redskins would swoop down out of Oklahoma to steal livestock and, now and then, burn down a house or barn. North Texas was a safe haven for outlaws who could race for the Oklahoma Territory when they needed to hide out. Every stranger was suspect, a potential enemy.

I remember once when Mama and I were walking into town a horseman came up behind us at a fast lope and we turned to see if it was an acquaintance. Mama quickly pulled me to her side and we stepped off the road to let him pass. As he rode by he touched his hat and said, "Howdy, Ma'am" and went on down the road and around a bend, out of sight. He was riding a really handsome horse, and I thought him a rather dashing figure of a man. I asked Mama if she knew him. "No," she said, "but I know who he is. That was Sam Bass."

As young as I was, I knew Sam Bass by reputation, and it wasn't a reputation of a Robin Hood (as I have since heard some people romanticize). He was as tough an outlaw as Texas ever had: a murderer, a train robber, and a bandit. It was another

ten years before his luck ran out during a shootout following
a bank robbery.

There was another time when some of our livestock disappeared and, after asking around the neighboring farms, we
learned that there had been raids on other farms also. Among
the livestock missing was a span of mules owned by a widow
of a Confederate soldier. Her fifteen-year-old son had had them
hitched to a plow and was cultivating some land. That noon
he left them in the field while he went home for dinner, and
when he returned, they were gone. The widow then sent her
son over to ask for Grandpa's help in finding her mules.

A posse was formed that afternoon to search for the widow's
mules and the other missing livestock. The posse rode out
to a densely wooded area where a creek ran between steep
banks. The men divided into two groups, and half rode one
embankment, searching the creek bed opposite, and the other
half rode the other side doing the same. It wasn't long before
they spotted a makeshift corral in a deep undercut in the bank.
The hiding place was almost hidden with overhanging green
tree branches and cut brush. In the corral were our cows, some
horses, and the widow's mules. No one was around, so the
posse hid out to wait for the rustlers' return. And sure enough,
late in the afternoon they rode in driving stolen livestock.

We were all waiting up to hear what the posse had found
and, when we heard Grandpa and Uncle Garley ride in, we
rushed outside to meet them. Grandpa told Sam to take his
horse and the cows on to the barn and started into the house.
I asked him if they found the cattle thieves, and he muttered
something about "they got away." Uncle Garley got a drink
at the well, talked to Grandma for a minute, and rode off
for town. We were curious to know more about the whole affair, but Grandma told us not to pester Grandpa with questions and be glad that our livestock had been returned. I
thought it was a shame that the rustlers escaped because now

they would be back to steal again. Grandpa did not mention it the next morning and we didn't pester him. Later that day some neighbor boys, my brother Albert, and I were hunting squirrels two or three miles from town. The dogs were on a hot trail, yelping and excited, and we were running fast to keep up with them. Suddenly we broke through to a clearing. Right in the middle of that clearing was a large oak tree, and hanging from that tree were three bodies. Not a pretty sight, I can tell you.

Our hunt was over and we streaked it for home. I hadn't before and I haven't since done such plain and fancy running as I did that afternoon.

I couldn't sleep that night, and for years afterward I had nightmares about those men swinging there with all those blowflies swarming around them, and the dogs jumping up and whining around the tree.

We didn't mention what we had seen to any of the folks. Instinctively we knew we had seen something that we should not have discovered and knew something that we were not supposed to know. And no one, *no one,* ever disputed Grandpa. He had said they got away.

4

# The Posse

I have heard, in the years since I was a youth, many tales of postwar activities of the Ku Klux Klan. I know that the men of Grapevine who participated in Klan raids were not as organized or dedicated to the Klan Code as those in the Deep South. There was no membership, as such, and I certainly do not remember anything about grand wizards, secret signs, or initiations. The men around Grapevine simply banded together to protect themselves against a military government that showed them no justice and gave aid and protection to those who harmed and threatened them, their families, and their property. They helped each other when there was a need and used the best available methods to get the job done. Sometimes wearing white was a lot more effective — and did less harm — than carrying a gun.

As the situation got worse and the Reconstruction governments in the South became more unjust and unmerciful, and as the lawlessness of many was protected by a government that condoned any act that punished the South and the southerners, more and more groups banded together to handle their own problems. To say that this was right or to argue that this was wrong depended on the individual problem that arose and the way it was solved. More and more there were self-appointed posses and white robed men riding out at night. And as this activity increased, the control was returning to the local land-owners and away from the military rulers, the state police, and the Reconstruction governments.

In 1870 there was a reward of $500 offered for information about any known Klansman or Klan activity. A group of state police rode into Grapevine, posted notices of this reward, and rode out. Uncle Garley was in town when the notice was posted and came out to the farm to tell Grandpa. They immediately left to attend a meeting.

There was one man in Grapevine, a relative newcomer to the community, who was a known abolitionist and a suspected spy for the state police. The people around there had been suspicious of him for some time and gave him a wide berth. Everyone felt that he wasn't above going after that reward. Sam was assigned to hang around the general store where our mail was delivered and watch for any official-looking mail addressed to the suspected informer. Sam was a young boy, sixteen or so, and it wasn't unusual to see boys of his age curious and nosey about the mail.

In those days the mail was put out on a long table at the general store, and the people sorted through it and found their own letters and packages. The mail table was a gathering place, and each mail delivery was a social event. Letters were shared and news exchanged. Sam met every mail delivery.

It wasn't long until the letter he was waiting for came. Sam slipped it in his shirt, nodded to Grandpa and some of his friends who were outside the store talking, and headed for Uncle Garley's office where they all met. In fact, half the men in town followed them; an outsider would have thought that the men of Grapevine had been struck down by an epidemic and were rushing to see the doctor.

The letter was from the government office in Fort Worth stating that they had received the information about KKK ac-tivities around Grapevine. It listed the names of the men whom he had reported to them as active Klansmen and said that the state police would be up in a few days to pick up these men. It thanked the informer and praised him for his civic responsibility and mentioned that, after his information had been checked out and verified, he would receive his reward. Grandpa's name was one of those listed.

At the next mail delivery Uncle Garley picked up a stack of mail, sorted through it for his own letters, and placed the remaining letters on the table. The informer's letter was returned in the stack, and they watched as he picked it up. He quickly put it in his pocket, but not before he saw the letters across it: KKK.

Many of Grandpa's friends had taken the ironclad oath in order to hold office and vote but took part in the resistance. These men had an inside track on rumors, shared what they learned, and served as lookouts. Grapevine, indeed, had an extensive "grapevine"; it went from back fence to back fence, street corner to street corner, field to field. These families had lived so long with threats and harassment that this seemed just one more problem to face. Certainly they couldn't leave their homes, en masse. Nearly every man in town was involved though only a few were named in the letter. They began their wait, watched the roads, and made plans to act—just in case.

Life went on as usual, with one exception: the informer suddenly left town. At least, he wasn't seen again after that day when he picked up his letter. A state policeman came asking for him, but no one knew what had happened to him or where he might have gone.

Late one afternoon, Sam and I were alone at the farm when a man from Grapevine rode up to our fence and asked to speak to Grandpa. When we told him he wasn't home he glanced over his shoulder, then leaned close and said, "Go find him and say that Tuck Boaz says to be prepared. Tell him company's comin' tomorrow." I quickly bridled a horse, rode out to the field where Grandpa was plowing, and gave him the message. The next day we had just finished dinner, and Grandpa was resting in the back room. The women were clearing the table, and we were out back on the porch. None of us heard the horses come down the lane and were completely taken by surprise when a posse of men surrounded the house. I rushed through the door in time to see Mr. Boaz and four men come through the front door. One of the men knocked Mama against the wall. I had never before seen anyone mistreat Mama and I made a lunge for him, flailing both arms. Mama grabbed me and shoved me behind her. There was confusion everywhere. Albert and Dick were kicking and biting, Grandma was flapping her apron, and Mama and my aunts were trying to protect Grandma and the children. I saw Mr. Boaz head right for the bedroom where Grandpa was. I took off after him.

When Grandpa heard the commotion he rolled off the bed and under it. He was a big man, several inches over six feet, and one foot was left sticking out from under the bed. Mr. Boaz saw it as soon as he came into the room. So did I. He gave Grandpa's foot a swift kick and muttered, "Get your foot hidden, you damn fool!"

He grabbed Grandpa's hat from the bedpost and threw it under the bed, whirled around, and ran out of the room yelling, "He's not here, boys. He got away. The kid, here, says he is headed for the territory. We can catch him if we hurry. Follow me!"

Like stampeding cattle, they all rushed out after Mr. Boaz, mounted, and took off after him, stirring up dust as they rode out of sight going north. I have often wondered how far they rode and how long they searched before they realized that Grandpa had given them the slip.

Grandpa left that night traveling light, riding fast, and going south.

# 5

# Toward Mexico

Grandpa wasn't at the breakfast table the next morning, and for the first time in my memory we did not get our individual instructions for the day. Grandpa had hitherto dictated our every move, made all decisions, told us what to think and believe. Until now, I had always thought of the Family as two sets: Grandpa and "the others." This morning I looked around the table and saw each person as an individual.

Uncle Garley had come over that morning and was sitting in Grandpa's place—lightning didn't strike! Uncle Garley, Aunt Mary Jane, and their three children had their own house in town. He had his practice, which kept him busy, but he kept cattle on our place. He expected us to take care of them, do all the chores, and follow his many, many orders—and without ever so much as a "thank you kindly." My brothers, Sam, and I did not favor him and kept our distance whenever possible.

Sam was my uncle but close enough to my age that he seemed more a brother. Until recently, he was just one of us kids, but I had been noticing that he was starting to shave out by the well and no longer played with us after church but joined the young crowd and talked to the girls. Albert, Dick, and I had discussed it among ourselves and resented that he was ordering us around and starting to act like Uncle Garley. Mama told us to pay him no mind, that he was just having growing pains.

I asked him once if he hurt and he just looked at me and walked off saying something about "you younguns."

Aunt Harriet was a second mother to us. She and Mama were the closest in age and constant companions. They were each other's confidante, shared a room, shared their clothes, worked their chores together. Both taught school. Aunt Harriet was thirty-three years old and resented being called an "old maid schoolteacher." She often had callers, and we knew not to go out on the front porch when she was entertaining, though Grandpa always did.

Aunt Matt was the sickly one. She walked with the crutches that Grandpa bought for her in Fort Worth. He also bought a surrey for the women to drive to church, which was easier for her to get into than the wagon. Being that baby who had survived the Alabama "vapor sickness," she had a special place in Grandma's heart and where Grandma was you usually found Aunt Matt.

Mama! Mama was the most beautiful woman I knew, with black, black hair, very fair skin, and the palest blue eyes you ever saw. She was taller than the other women I knew, very strict with her children, and we wanted more than anything to please her. I never remember a time that she was unkind or unjust. She was our bulwark against grandparents, aunts, and uncles who were too demanding, too sharp and impatient with "that brood of Nan's who were always underfoot."

Grandma was the one we took for granted, that woman in the kitchen who told us to "go ask your Grandpa" when we asked her a question and when we asked him something said, "Don't pester your Grandpa." It never occurred to me that she ever had a thought of her own or could survive if Grandpa was not around to direct her every thought and move. Now I saw her in a different light. Grandma was in charge—even Uncle Garley recognized this—and she wore her mantle of authority well. We were all amazed.

She told us that morning we were going to move to Mexico

where there was a settlement of Confederates who had gone there after the end of the war. Some families from East Texas were there with whom she and Grandpa had corresponded. She said Grandpa had gone ahead and would meet us down the trail with a guide and an interpreter. She told Uncle Garley to let it be known that our farm was for sale. The rest of us were to go about our business as usual, keep our ears open, and our mouths shut.

By the time she found a buyer for the farm, she had sold most of the small animals and much of our equipment and furniture. What we didn't sell we gave to friends, though there were few who were not leaving also. There was quite an exodus from Grapevine that spring and summer. Several other families were planning to go to Mexico, and we planned to travel together—not leave together, but meet on down the line.

Grandma cried just once when she gave away her solid walnut wardrobe, which she had moved from South Carolina to Alabama to East Texas to Grapevine. All the Family broke down then, and it took some time to get everyone to stop crying.

We were sad to be leaving. We had lived there eight years and had many friends. The saddest part was leaving Johnny Statem behind.

Johnny Statem was an orphan boy who had come to live with us. He was about my age or a few years older. The Family wanted to take him with us, but as our plans progressed it became evident that this was impractical. Johnny owned some property his family had left to him. Grandma couldn't sell it for him, and he would have lost it if he had gone to Mexico with us. Johnny was to stay behind and live with the neighbor who bought our surrey; but we didn't know that until just before we left.

Late one afternoon Grandma asked Johnny to walk with her down to the creek. When they returned Johnny told us that he was going to stay in Grapevine and take care of our surrey. He knew that Grandma was proud of this surrey, which was the finest one in the area, black with red wheels and fringe around the canopy. Johnny liked to drive it and took his turn with the other boys when we drove it to church. We never saw Johnny again after we left Grapevine, but we often talked about him and that surrey. I'll bet he took real good care of it.

At last we had everything packed into three wagons. Somehow Grandma had received word from Grandpa that he would meet us south of Waco. Uncle Garley traveled with us until we joined other wagons south of Fort Worth. Then he returned to Grapevine.

That first morning we passed by the Lonesome Dove Cemetery. Mama and I climbed out of the wagon and ran to my brother Tommy's grave. Tommy had died of pneumonia four years earlier when he was just ten years old. I had been to his gravesite many times with Mama and Aunt Mary Jane, who also had a child buried there next to Tommy. Her child's grave had a headstone, but Tommy's grave was unmarked, just covered with a sandstone slab. Mama had planned that someday she would put up a marker with his name on it. Now she realized that she might never get a chance to do so.

She asked for my jackknife and I handed it to her, thinking that she was going to trim back some Johnson grass around the sandstone slab. To my distress, she used my knife to scratch into the soft stone:

T. R. V. 1859–1869

She ruined my knife but I did not try to stop her. She was crying hard as she worked, bearing down as she cut in a deep groove. When she finished we just stood there — for a long time it seemed to me. I began to fidget as I realized that the wagons were almost out of sight, just a cloud of dust down the road. I took her hand and whispered, "Mama, Mama, they are going off and leaving us. We have to go now." She hugged me; then we started running after the wagons. I didn't look back.

I had the sensation that Tommy was running after us, falling farther and farther behind until he wasn't there any more. When we caught up with the wagons, Mama said, "Don't look back, Mac." I wondered if she had the same vision I had.

(Mama often expressed a wish to go back to "check on little Tommy's plot to see if it is in good condition." She never got to return, and over fifty years passed before I did. That same piece of sandstone lay among the blades of Johnson grass, and I could clearly read the letters made by my jackknife. Nearby was the stone that read "Babe Dial." I closed my eyes and felt Mama's presence beside me, heard the dove calling from a nearby tree, and heard the wagons rumbling down the road.)

We traveled as fast as we could, the horses setting the pace. We took the back trails, cutting down through Ellis, Navarro, and Limestone counties. Often my uncle lagged behind to check if we were being followed. This move was not the lark that the move from East Texas had seemed. I took my turn at driving the wagons, making camp, hunting game, and repairing our equipment. I was twelve that summer of 1873, the man of my family. I had my responsibilities: Mama and my two younger brothers.

We joined up with two other families and met Grandpa near Salado. He had hired a guide who claimed he spoke Spanish and could help us settle in Mexico. It wasn't long before we knew that he was a poor guide. We suspected he stole money from Grandpa, and when we met a family of Mexicans on the road, we realized he knew only a few words of Spanish. He had started asking too many questions about our reasons for moving to Mexico. Grandpa decided to run him off. He had been paid a hundred dollars as part of his fee. He demanded more but did not get it. We were relieved when he left and headed back to Waco, disgruntled and shouting threats.

At Bastrop we stopped for several weeks. Grandpa and the other men bought a crop and harvested it. The women put up fruits and vegetables, kept what we could for our own use, and sold the rest. There was much to do to repair our wagons, feed up our animals, and rest them for the journey ahead. Late in the fall we moved on south.

Once, I remember that we camped near a river; it was a really beautiful place, just south of Austin. The next morning, Mama and I decided to start before the wagons were ready and walk on ahead. The fall morning was cool and the trees made flickering shadows and sunlit patches on the winding road that followed the creek bed. I was enjoying a contentment and peace of mind that I hadn't felt in many months. This was my special time with Mama, something that she managed to have with each of her boys as often as she could.

We were walking along by ourselves, talking about our plans for a new and different life, wondering about our friends back home. She told me about her girlhood on the plantation in Alabama and how she met Papa when she taught school near his store in New Danville. By midmorning the sun began to bear down; the road had left the creek bed and was running across a prairie. We were getting thirsty and warm and so began looking around for shade where we could rest and wait for the wagons. Mama pointed ahead to a lone cabin under some trees and suggested we wait there for our party to catch up with us.

We had thought the place was deserted but, as we approached it, we saw clothes hanging on a fence behind the cabin and a young girl standing by a well under the trees. As we walked up to her a woman came out of the house and stood watching us. Neither seemed alarmed, just curious. Mama called to the woman and asked if we might have a drink of water and rest under their trees. The child took a dipper from a nail on the tree and dipped it into a bucket of water that she had been drawing as we walked up. She picked up another bucket and carried it over to the cabin, stood talking with the woman for a few minutes, then came running back toward us calling, "Ma says you can stay with us iffen you got no place to live."

I gasped and Mama pulled me toward her. The thin veneer

of security I had imagined that morning had peeled away and I saw, all too clearly, our true situation. We didn't have a place to live; we were homeless wanderers. My world never looked blacker than it did that moment.

Mama waved to the mother of the girl and thanked her, calling that we were with a wagon train that would be along shortly. The woman walked over to wait with us. She told us there had been some Indian raids to the north and she had thought we were some of the refugees she had seen come through, looking for a place to resettle. She was younger than my mother, and pregnant. She said her husband had gone into Austin for supplies. We heard a baby cry and she went into the cabin and came back with a little boy about two. We stood there talking until the wagons came into view. Mama and I went out to the road and hopped into the back of our wagon and waved as long as that hospitable family was in sight.

Mama saw to it that we continued our lessons; she was very strict on this point. Every day we had to write and cipher and read to her from our only books — the Bible and a leather-covered Latin grammar. We read every notice that was posted beside the road, and Dick, Albert, and I had spelling bees with the rest of the Family. We found an old newspaper beside the road, and we all studied it because we knew that Grandpa would take the spelling words from it. We were very competitive, and our spelling contests were main events around the campfire at night.

Mama drew on everything she could remember to help her educate her sons. She taught us history, government, law, literature, and astronomy without the aid of books. We would lie out under the stars at night, and she would point out the constellations and tell us stories of Greek mythology. I thought that my mother was the smartest, the most wonderful person in the world — and I still think she might well have been.

There was an election in the fall that the grown-ups followed closely. They discussed it much among themselves, and it was a main subject when we met strangers on the road and stopped to exchange news. We had traveled close by the capitol in Austin, and in that area there was little other discussed than the governor's race between Richard Coke and that most despised Union army soldier, that Radical, Governor E. J. Davis. Grandpa hated Davis and admired Coke and, of course, we took our cue from him. When the returns were in and Mr. Coke was the winner by a large majority, Grandpa rejoiced and canceled our plans to live in Mexico.

With this change in the political climate it was felt that the problems of the people of Texas would moderate. We had traveled as far as Cuero, Texas, when we halted our hegira to Mexico and settled in to winter around the wastelands near the Gulf. We pitched in and built a house — not much of a place but enough to shelter the nine of us. Some slept in the wagons when the weather permitted, and we did most of our cooking out-of-doors. The weather was mild, and we were glad to stay in one place for awhile. We were wishing that by spring we could turn around and return to home and friends — at least to some spot we could call our own and start to build our lives again.

In January, 1874, when the day came for Richard Coke to take office as the new Texas governor, there was trouble in Austin. The Davis forces declared the election unconstitutional and refused to admit defeat. E. J. Davis and a company of his state police occupied the first floor of the state capitol building and held it at gunpoint. Davis telegraphed President U. S. Grant requesting that he send federal troops to protect him and reinstate his cabinet. The answer came back from the president: Texas had been readmitted to the Union in 1870 and, as a state of the Union, must manage her own internal affairs. Grant wisely suggested to Davis that he retire from the field, and that night he and his all-Negro bodyguard of state police quietly slipped out of Austin.

One of the first acts of the new governor of Texas was to disband the hated state police. Grandpa began to make his plans in earnest.

There were family conferences held to discuss our situation. Our money and our supplies were low. We did not own the land where we were living; you might call us "squatters." Grandma called us "gypsies." She kept worrying that if we didn't locate soon where we could plant a crop and grow a garden we would all starve to death. Uncle Garley had written urging us to leave "that mosquito-infested malaria country." Albert had been sick ever since we settled there, and Grandma worried about a return of the "vapor sickness" that had caused the deaths of her children. She joined the others urging Grandpa to make a decision.

The children begged to return to Grapevine but Grandpa said that he would not feel safe there, not yet anyhow. He and Grandma were approaching their seventies and they yearned for a safe haven where they could find rest and peace. My aunts wanted to marry, to have homes and families of their own. Mama wanted security and futures for her sons. Sam and Grandpa, my brothers and I talked of nothing else but finding a spot where we could raise cattle — somewhere with open ranges.

Grandpa left in the early spring to meet with Uncle Garley and find a place to homestead. When they returned we were waiting, packed and ready to pull out. They had claimed land in Comanche County and we moved there, near Blanket, Texas. We moved in May. I was thirteen years old.

6

# The Farm

We settled in time to plant Grandma's garden. We pitched in and cleared land, got in the summer crops, built a house, barn, corral, and fences. That fall, Sam and I went by horseback to Grapevine and brought back our herd, which we had left there with Uncle Garley. They had been *our* cattle when we left them there a little over a year before. Now he gave us long and definite orders as how to take care of *his* cattle until he moved to Comanche County the next summer. I knew Grandpa would straighten him out as soon as he heard that. He did.

I did not return to school in the fall as my younger brothers did. Grandpa, Sam, and I did the work around the farm. There was some harvesting to do, the cattle to work, furniture to build, the house to weather in. In the spring there was planting to do, and we began to build up our herd.

In the early summer of 1875 our Tennessee kin came to visit. We were sitting on the porch about sunset on a Sunday afternoon when three wagons turned up our lane. Visitors were a rarity; everyone rushed to the gate, excited and curious. When the wagons pulled to a halt the men and women in them jumped down and rushed to the rear to assist an old man who had started to climb out of his wagon even before it stopped. I thought that little man was the most dried up, the most antiquated specimen I had ever seen. We could hear his argumentative, high-pitched voice screeching, "Leave me alone . . . get your hands off me . . . get away, get away, all of you!"

Then Grandma pushed past us calling, "Alex, Alex, you have come to see me. Oh, children, it is Brother Alex." It was Alexander Patton, Jr.

He was her brother whom she hadn't seen in over forty years. For the next several minutes there was crying, laughing, and introductions going on all at the same time. There was Uncle Alex with several of his children, their husbands and wives, children and two babies. I wasn't sure if the babies were grandchildren or great-grandchildren but there was someone of every age. They had come out west to find land to homestead—and to visit their Texas kin.

Alex Patton was definitely the bellwether of his family. They jumped to do his every command, and he could set Grandpa to shame when it came to giving orders. As guest of honor, he was given the best bed in the best room. He retired early and his daughters took his supper up to him on a tray.

After supper the children played games to release their pent-up energy. They had been on the trail for weeks. The grownups sat on the porch and visited. Mama hadn't seen these cousins since she was a young girl. I sat at the end of the porch and watched them visit. They were all talking at once and laughing. Mama looked happy and pretty.

The next morning Grandma sent me to wake Uncle Alex and to take him some hot water. I knocked on the door and heard him call out in that high, whiny voice, "Well, come on in, come on in. Don't just stand there hammering on the door."

I looked in and thought at first there was no one in bed. He was so small he hardly made a bulge in the covers. He sat up and ordered me, "Son, reach under this bed and hand me that jug and tin cup."

I retrieved the jug and cup for him, then stood back and

stared. He poured himself a full cup of corn liquor and downed it raw. One of his daughters came in with a cup of strong, black coffee, and he used that as a chaser. Next he reached over to the sidetable and took a plug of tobacco and gnawed off a chunk with his toothless gums.

I backed out of that room still not believing what I had seen.

After I knew him a little better, I asked him, "Uncle Alex, how long have you been hitting that jug, downing black coffee, and chewing tobacco?"

"Since I was fifteen, young feller, and that's the reason I have lived so long. Whiskey, tobacco, and coffee never hurt anyone."

I had just had my fourteenth birthday and I didn't think in just one more year I would be ready to follow his prescription for longevity. He must have been about eighty then and lived several more years.

Uncle Garley, Aunt Mary Jane, and their five children moved to Comanche County that summer. For a while we all lived together on the farm. There were sixteen of us in the Family. The recent additions were: Belle, older than I; Willie, just a few months my junior; Andrew Jackson, eight years old; Audrey, three years old; and Roy, one year. The quarters were close, and Dick and I found a corner in the barn where we preferred to bed down rather than crowd our way in every night. Albert slept on the sleeping porch. The barn made him cough. He had not been well since we had lived down on the Texas coast.

Since my brothers and I had no father, all the adults in the Family considered it their duty and privilege to discipline us and give us orders. I guess we had more bosses than just about anyone. Mama was constantly arbitrating family disputes, soothing hurt feelings, cooling the fiery tempers of her sons, her brothers, her nephews, and her father. It bothered Mama, no little, that she and her sons worked so hard, shouldered their share of the problems and responsibilities, but were considered less than full partners in the Family ventures and fortunes. The misfortunes? In those we had full share.

One day one of Uncle Garley's sons made a remark that Mama recognized as a quote of something he had overheard from his elders. The gist of it was that the Vernon boys should do a larger share of the work to earn their keep because they were "dependents of the Family." He made the remark to me, but Mama heard him and it brought to surface all the hurt and resentment she had built up over twelve years.

Everyone was home that afternoon and stood back in shock as "quiet, forbearing, meek Nan—Nan the peacemaker" exploded like a volcano. She marched past us on her way to the barn and hitched up a wagon and team. While she loaded in our clothes and some bedding, Grandma fluttered around wringing her hands and Grandpa kept saying, "Now, Nan, don't be hasty . . . don't be rash . . . you know you belong here with us." Sam and Uncle Garley found chores to do, down back of the barn; Aunt Matt and Aunt Harriet stood around and cried.

When she was ready Mama climbed up on the wagon, took up the reins, and called to her sons. We rode off down the road to Blanket—Mama, Albert, Dick, and I. We found a little house, not much more than a shack, and moved in that night. This was the first home of our own, that I could remember, and I thought it a palace.

The next morning Grandpa came in to see us. He and Mama talked out by the gate for a long time, then he rode off. Later he came back with the wagon. There was one of our milk cows tied behind and some chickens in the wagon. Uncle Garley and Sam were with him, and they stayed until dark making repairs on the house and building a pen for the chickens. There was a shed out back for the cow. As they left Grandpa said, "Your mother expects you Sunday for dinner."

There was no lasting schism. We visited often at the farm, helped out when there was a need, and they always stopped by our house when any of them came to town. But we never again lived with the Family.

# 7

# Blanket, Texas

We made it just fine without the Family's help. Mama taught at the school my brothers attended. After school, Albert and Dick did odd jobs in return for the supplies that we needed and did not grow in our garden. I was nearly fifteen and a big kid for my age. The ranchers around Blanket hired me on as an extra hand when they needed help. Most of the time I lived where I was working; that helped Mama as there was one less mouth to feed.

How much money did I get? I thought I was making good pay. I got three dollars a month and my board and keep. Sometimes I was furnished a horse so I could ride to and from home.

We had good neighbors, the Daldt Cooks. They had lived in Blanket for many years when we moved next door. They helped us start our garden, looked in on Albert when he was sick and Mama was away at her teaching job, furnished us with milk when our cow went dry. My brothers and I helped Daldt chop his wood, helped with their milking, and ran errands for Mrs. Cook. Daldt was just about my best friend. Once he gave me a dime for finding his cow that had wandered off. It was the first coin I had ever owned, and Mama said that I could keep it. I spent it to buy her a present for her forty-third birthday that November of 1876.

I had another good friend whom I made after we moved

into Blanket. Arch Davis was about ten years older than I and sort of took me under his wing. He worked as a cowboy on the ranches in the area. He helped me get jobs, taught me to brand cattle, and made a farm boy into a cowboy. I guess I had a case of hero worship when it came to Arch.

A man I had worked for moved out to Trickham, Texas, south of Coleman—said he wanted to get away from fences. He hired my friend, Arch Davis, to be his top hand, and Arch asked me if I wanted to go too. We rode out to talk to Mr. Jones, and he hired me. I told him that I would be at his new ranch in about two weeks. He and Arch were leaving for Trickham that day, but I had a job that I had to finish and I knew that Mama was not going to agree to my moving so far away—not right off, at least.

It was a week before I could muster enough nerve to tell Mama, and she took it just as I thought she would. First she said, "No!" Then in a few days said, "I'll think on it and talk to Grandpa." She moped around there all week, and we couldn't find much to say to one another. My brothers followed close at my heels, and we talked about their responsibilities after I left.

The Saturday night before I was to leave, I was sitting on the front steps and Mama came out and sat beside me, took my hand, and said, "All right, Mac, if you really want to try your wings, I understand." Mama always understood.

I left in the late afternoon on a Sunday. I should have gotten an earlier start, but I kept hanging around finding things to do. I think Mama thought that I had changed my mind and I nearly did several times. Finally, I got down my bedroll and started rolling in my few possessions. Mama came in, patted me aside, and rearranged my packing. She went out to the kitchen and put up some grub for me to take along on the overnight trip.

I saddled the horse that Arch had left with me, told Mama, Albert, and Dick good-bye, and started off. I could not look back but I knew they were standing by the gate as long as I was in sight. Later, I heard a bird call and I thought it was Mama coming after me and calling, "Mac! Mac!" If I had seen her when I jerked around, I would have gone home, for sure.

I rode until dark, then stopped under a big tree, made camp, and ate the cold biscuits and meat Mama had given me. I was never so lonesome in my life. I missed Mama, my brothers, and the Family. I was trying to be the brave adult that I thought I had become but, all at once, I couldn't hold back the flood of tears that had been held in check since I was a small boy. I lay there on the ground, beat my fists against the tree, and cried as hard as anyone could. No one was there to witness my disgrace, and I cried until I was exhausted. Then I rolled up in my blanket and hiccupped myself to sleep.

The next morning I rode on in and started the job with Mr. Jones and Arch. It was in the spring of 1877, just before my sixteenth birthday.

8

# Arch Davis

Mr. Jones had only the two of us working for him, Arch and me. The three of us did everything that had to be done on the place, and since it was a new ranch there was a lot to do. Arch and I worked well together, and I was really enjoying my new life, doing what I liked best—work with cattle.

It wasn't long before Arch knew all the people around Trickham. He was as friendly as a puppy, and the women thought him right handsome. One husband dubbed him "the local ladies' man." Maybe that man had reason to be jealous. I don't know. Arch never talked to me about his social life. As good friends as we were, there was still that ten years' age difference and I just wasn't in his league when it came to sporting around town.

One morning at breakfast Arch told me about a wolf he had seen on the northern edge of our range where he was working that week. Arch owned a pistol but he thought he might get a better shot at the wolf with my Winchester. He asked if he could take my gun with him that day. I sure wanted the wolf killed, and I was pleased that I had something Arch wanted to borrow.

I was moving hay into the barn that morning, so I stayed home. Arch tied the rifle behind his saddle and rode off.

Late in the afternoon Arch rode into town for a beer before

coming home. He still had my Winchester so, rather than leave it outside tied to his saddle, he carried it into the saloon with him.

I have wondered many times: if he hadn't been blinded by the sudden change in light between the sun outside and the dim light inside . . . if he hadn't been carrying my rifle . . . if only I had been with him. But fate deemed otherwise. When he went through those swinging saloon doors, that drunken, jealous husband shot Arch right through the head.

Trickham had no hospital or even a doctor to come to his aid in time. The men who saw the shooting put him in a buckboard and brought him out to the ranch; there was nothing else they could do for him.

Arch was in bad shape. We couldn't keep a bandage on his head so I sat there for hours, wiping the blood and ooze that came through the big hole in his forehead. He would doze, then talk. He rambled about his home, people he knew, things that had happened in his childhood, plans for his future.

Late in the night a buggy drove up to the house and a young woman knocked on the screen door. She was the wife of the man who had shot Arch. She came in and sat beside Arch for the rest of the night. I left them alone and went out and sat on the porch steps. I could hear them talking low but I did not hear what they said to each other. Just after daylight she came out crying, got into her buggy, and rode off.

I went in and Arch was dead.

Arch Davis had been my good friend and buddy. After his death I knew that I did not want to remain around Trickham. Mr. Jones and I made a trade and I selected a saddle and horse for part of the wages he owed me. With my horse, my Winchester, my bedroll, and a few dollars, I rode out of Trickham and headed for home.

I stayed with Mama and the boys for two weeks. It was the summer of 1880. We were out at the farm when the census taker came around.

I had made my plans before I left Trickham to go west and try my luck on some of the big ranches. I wanted to be a cowboy like the ones I had seen at the stockyards in Abilene, the ones that rode for the big outfits. I wanted to learn the cattle business.

I rode out of Blanket in September. I am sure Mama was concerned about my leaving with no destination in mind, but she didn't show it. I was excited and felt confident. I knew just as much about ranch work as any man — I thought — and somewhere there was a place where I could work and be happy — I was sure of it. I turned my horse to the west.

9

# Half Circle Six

In San Angelo I was told that a company named J. I. Case Heirs had bought one of the large spreads in the area. They were planning to build up their herds and were hiring experienced hands. I considered myself an experienced hand so I rode out to Knickerbocker where they had their headquarters on the head of Dove Creek.

The farther I rode into the ranch and the more I saw of that big operation, the less experienced and less confident I felt. By the time I reached the ranch headquarters, I felt so young, green, and inadequate that I almost lost my nerve and bolted. If I hadn't come so far and been so hungry and tired, I would have turned around and headed back to Blanket.

I rode up to a fence and sat there on my horse watching some roping and branding. I didn't know where to go or what to do next, and I was relieved when a man walked over and asked me what I wanted. I told him that I was looking for work and, without waiting for him to answer, reeled off my experience. I was scared and he knew it.

He asked how old I was and I answered, "Twenty-one." He stood there for a minute looking at the ground. When he looked up I thought he was going to tell me to leave, but he said to stable my horse at a barn that he pointed out. Next he called to one of the boys, told him to show me where to bunk and to bring me around to see him after supper. I had been talking to the ranch foreman.

That evening he asked me again how old I was. This time I answered, "Nearly twenty." He smiled, nodded, and said, "Well, let's see what you can do." I knew then if I had lied again he would not have hired me.

For the next eight years I worked for the Stilson, Case, Thorp, Ryburn Company on their ranch called the Half Circle Six. I gained the reputation of being a top hand, built up my own little herd, sent money home, and saved a little. Cowpunching was hard work but work I enjoyed, and I found life interesting. Each season on a ranch makes its own demands. Most days are much alike. Those eight years flow together as a single period in my life and I cannot remember things chronologically. There is much that I have forgotten. But some of my experiences stand out in my memory more clearly than others, and I can see them in my mind's eye as if I were living through them again.

PART TWO

# Young Man Riding with the Big Boys

10

# The Army Contractor

A man near Eagle Pass had a contract with the army to supply beef to them; he did not raise cattle and was not buying from any of the ranches. The ranch owners suspected that the only way he could meet his orders was with stolen cattle.

Identifying stolen cattle, once located, was a simple matter. None of the large outfits sold cattle locally. They sent cattle to market or butchered cows for their own use. Calves were branded and kept until they were sent to market or butchered, or they were raised and kept for breeding. You can sum it up this way: as long as a hide had a brand on it, and that brand wasn't on a hide in a packing house, it belonged to the ranch running that brand. It was as simple as that.

The ranch owners made up a party of about twenty-five cowhands—men from the larger ranches and some from several of the smaller spreads. I was sent along from the Half Circle Six. Our assignment was to check out the herd of the army supplier and look for the brands belonging to the ranches we represented. We traveled in groups of two or three and joined up just east of Del Rio.

One of the boys had gone ahead, posing as a "waddy" out of a job. He had located the herd, and when we met him in Del Rio he took us right out to the pasture owned by the army contractor. There was only one section under fence. That much pasture in the area wouldn't support ten cows, but he had over two hundred head there. Our precautions to keep our investigation a secret must have worked because he was there alone and taken completely by surprise.

We took him along with us to his salt grounds and called up his cattle.

I was the youngest of the bunch and, I guess, feeling overly conscientious and important as a representative of the Half Circle Six. I was too green to know caution at that point. I made the first move.

Right off I spotted a cow with Doc Brown's brand. Doc Brown had nursed me through a bad case of black measles the winter before, and I felt very beholden to him. I turned to the contractor and asked him how he had come to have that cow. He replied that he had bought several steers from a man on Devil's River and he thought that was one of them. I cut him off with, "You are a liar. That cow belongs to Doc Brown and I'm taking it back to San Angelo."

I rode in to cut it out, and he came after me swinging a rope. Frank King, a man with plenty of nerve and a good friend of mine, took after him, poked a .45 in his ribs, and said, "Mister, you had better leave that kid alone." Frank held him over on the side while twenty-six pairs of eyes went over the herd.

When we finished cutting out our brands, there were not more than twenty head left. We recognized some of the remaining cows as having been stolen but they belonged to the outfits too chintzy to share the expense of the investigation or send a man along to help. We rode off with our recovered stock and left the contractor standing beside his open gate, cursing and screaming threats.

We stayed around that area several days, looking over other herds along the border. Once the word got out that we were inspecting brands, many rustlers took their stolen cattle over into Mexico. But when we started for home we were driving three hundred head back to our ranges.

Funny thing about cattle thieves of the era: they would bunch together for self-protection (and to steal from each other) and cluster around the edges of the big cattle company ranges— say, between the Matadors and the Spur ranches. I am not naming any towns, but I have several in mind that have more than their share of low-down, ornery, thieving citizens. You know, the kind folks refer to as mean and tough. If you will remember that these towns sprang up near the big cattle outfits and the founders were mostly cattle rustlers, it stands to reason that their children and even grandchildren averaged out a sorry lot.

# 11

# "Lord" Vernon

After the Civil War there were more than a few English, Scotch, and Canadians who settled in West Texas, and many of them built first-rate spreads. There was a big ranch near us owned by Canadians. It was run like a military outpost—very strict and very regimented. Most of the hands were Canadians and they were housed in a two-story, barracks-like building instead of bunkhouses. Once I was caught out in a blizzard and spent the night there. They were nice enough to me but standoffish and stiff; I wasn't comfortable.

The Matador Ranch was owned by a Scotchman and the Buena Ventura Ranch was owned by an Englishman.

This Englishman came to Abilene by train and to San Angelo by stage. I happened to be in town when he arrived on the stage. I don't know what had happened to make the driver so testy, but I could tell by the way he threw down all of the fine luggage that he wasn't in the best of moods. After he tossed down the last trunk and started walking away, one passenger ordered him to move the luggage out of the street and onto the walk. When the driver kept going and then started climbing onto the stage, this passenger pulled himself to his full height and said, "My good man, do you know who I am? I am the Honorable William Vernon, son of a lord."

The driver let go a sluice of tobacco juice right at his feet and snarled back, "I don't care if you are the son of the Lord, the Lord himself, or the Pope. If you want that pile of hides anyplace else you can move it there yourself." With that he climbed onto the stage, flapped the reins, and rode out of town.

After that we called him "Lordy-Lordy" and, I am sure, made no special effort to understand him. He or his family must have been wealthy, for he bought up a lot of land and stocked it with fine sheep. He fenced in his property and ran his sheep on open range as well. He built a fine house, fancy barns, and even a gatehouse. He rode a big, black English Hunter with a postage-stamp saddle anchored just behind the shoulders. He would ride by, stiff as a poker, and never return a "Howdy," just looked straight ahead as if you had insulted him by speaking. When he rode up to his gatehouse, he expected his boys to run open the gate and bow as he rode through. One of his ex-hands told me he quit because "he wanted us to be his damn vassals and go 'round curtsying."

He staged the first "fox" hunt ever held in Texas for some guests he entertained from England. They chased a coyote and made their poor horses jump barbed-wire fences. Several horses were so cut up they had to be shot. Anyone who mistreated their horses rated pretty low on our scale.

Just the fact that he built so many fences and ran sheep was enough to make any cowman dislike him. That country was open range land, and there were times when we drove our cattle through his territory, and we did not go out of our way to avoid his flocks. Always, the evening after we had scattered his sheep, "Lord" Vernon would ride over to our camp to protest. We would expect him, and when he came into view, prancing on his big, black hunter, some smart mouth would sing out, "Mac, here comes your 'cousin.'"

He would protest, make his threats, and glare down at us like we were ants on the ground. We would beg his pardon and say that our cattle had stampeded again. I am sure he reported us to headquarters, but Mr. Ryburn never once said anything to us.

He stayed several years, then sold out and returned to England. But it was a long time before I heard the last of "your cousin" from the other boys.

# Shootin' and Singin'

We were on a spring roundup, this time out around Pecos. At night, before we turned in, it was our habit to do a little blanket gambling. On one particular evening we were playing monte with a Mexican deck. The stakes were small. As I recall, the pot that caused all the trouble contained less than a dollar; in fact, I remember that it was exactly fifty cents.

Jim played a trey and held his thumb over one spot so the card would appear to be a deuce. He declared himself a winner and started gathering up the cards on the blanket. Ed Slone, the loser of that pot, called his hand and grabbed the cards before they could be mixed together. He unmasked Jim's attempt to cheat and a fight started. We separated them, but not before Ed picked up a quirt and hit Jim over the head with the butt end.

Jim was dazed, and I know that the blow really hurt him. We had to help him with his bedroll, and I was concerned about him and that lump on his head. None of us had much sympathy with a card cheat but we were plenty disgusted with them both. The game ended and we all turned in.

Jim wouldn't get up the next morning, said his head hurt and he wasn't going to work that day. We rode off, leaving him alone at the camp.

Late in the afternoon we rode in with a large herd. The camp was at the foot of a low, rolling hill, and just as we started toward the camp we heard rifle shots. Jim was taking shots at Ed, who was riding on the far side of the herd and about a hundred yards from camp.

Ed grabbed a Colt .45 out of his saddlebag and fell to the ground. He started running low, using the herd as a shield. When the bullets started whistling over the heads of those cows, they separated into two columns, leaving Ed right in the center of an open lane about fifty feet across. When Ed realized that he had no cover, he turned and charged toward Jim.

I was riding at the rear of the herd, still up on the rise of the hill and looking right down the center of that corridor. It was the dangdest sight I had ever seen. Those cows were flanking that space as if they were being held in place by a fence, and Jim was at one end, lying prone, pumping his rifle and firing at Ed, and Ed was running, crouched and zigzagging, holding his .45 in both hands. I expected him to go down at any moment. At about forty feet Ed's hat was shot off. When that happened Ed stopped, took aim, and shot once. Jim was killed instantly.

The whole tragedy happened so fast that none of us could have stopped it. We just sat there stunned. Probably from the first to the last shot was less than two minutes, but remembering about it now, events seemed to roll in slow motion.

After the shooting stopped, the cattle closed ranks. The others rushed in to see to Jim, and I rode forward to check on Ed. He was sitting there on the ground, with the cattle milling around him, punching out the empty shell and reloading his pistol. He was in shock and deadly calm. I took him by the arm and walked him out of the herd before they trampled him.

Ed and two of the boys took Jim's body back to headquarters. There was an investigation, and Ed was exonerated. He had acted in self-defense, pure and simple. Ed had quit the outfit by the time I returned from roundup, and I never saw him again.

Many years later, I heard of an Ed Slone who owned a nice spread in West Texas. I wondered, when I heard that name, if that was the same fellow who had come so near losing his life over a four-bit bet.

There was another shooting at a line camp near one of ours on the Rocking Chair Range. One of the boys who was there told us about it a week after it happened. It was triggered by just as trivial a thing as that monte game.

They had been out for several weeks on roundup. When the stretch is too long, the weather unfavorable, and the work monotonous, it takes very little to set everyone grumbling. The food and the cooking are usually the first complaints. Camp biscuits are made with water, about as tasteless as clay and as hard as a saddle on a long day's ride. Everyone, everywhere, grumbled about the camp biscuits.

One morning, John Chance said that he refused to eat the biscuits another time. He took a bucket and rode over to a squatter's shack about two miles away. He bought some buttermilk and rode the two miles back to camp. That sounds easier than it is. You have to hold the bucket on the saddle horn, balancing it as you gentle your horse over rocks and gullies, all the time trying to keep it from sloshing. You are lucky if you get back with half the amount you started with. John's clothes were sour and smelling of buttermilk by the time he handed the cook the bucket and took off to find the other wranglers, who were already at work.

All day long he talked about the biscuits they would have for supper. He was as excited as if he was going to a turkey dinner at a Christmas party. He was the last to ride in that evening, and the other boys were already sitting around waiting for chow call. As soon as John dismounted, the cook called him over to the chuckwagon and showed him the empty bucket. Someone had ridden in early and drunk the buttermilk. The cook swore that he had not done the drinking, but he wouldn't tell who had.

John swung around, marched over to his bedroll, and pulled his rifle from it. He turned to the others, who were sitting propped against the wagon, and said, "Which one of you is the son-of-a-bitch who drank my buttermilk?"

One of the hands started rising as he said, "I drank that g–ddamn buttermilk and I'm not taking that name off any-one." He lunged for John and John shot him. He killed him.

John threw his bedroll across the back of his horse and mounted. Just as he rode off he said to the others, who were staring at him in stunned silence, "If there is anyone else who wants some buttermilk, you can go get it yourself."

No one followed him, and he was never heard of again.

Some fifty years after this happened, a friend of mine who had heard me tell this story repeated it to a rancher in Llano County, Texas. This rancher said that he had been told the same tale by another man, and when he had heard it the first time, he suspected that the teller was the gunman. He hadn't ad-mitted it exactly, but the inference was there. If this was in-deed the case, then John Chance settled in Llano County, raised a family, led a very respectable life, and died of old age — under an assumed name.

Speaking of cooks — I never knew one who was very popu-lar. Generally, they were a disgruntled, grouchy lot. We had one who never had a pleasant word to say to any of us. After supper, instead of joining the group for a smoke and talk, he would go off and read his Bible. Don't misunderstand me — nothing wrong with that — but it was his holier-than-thou atti-tude and unfriendliness that made us all dislike him. Once he called me a "dom liar." I knocked him down and held my heel on his throat till he took it back. One of the boys made up a song about him that he sang on night guard. It went something like this:

> The cook he reads from a very big book
> But I think he's somewhat of a quack
> He thinks that some day he'll fly away
> With a pair of wings on his back.

We had one Chinese cook who was all right, and we liked him about as well as any. One day I was riding back to camp late in the afternoon. I saw a cloud of dust rolling toward me and in the center of it was our cook, riding bareback with only a rope hackamore for a bridle. He was going full speed, switching his horse on one rump then the other and bouncing so you could see daylight under him. I turned, galloped beside him, and yelled, "What's the matter, Ching? Where are you going?"

He never slowed down but yelled back, "Ching go town, me bitey one vinegaroon!"

He rode on, and I turned around and headed for camp to see what had happened to him. I learned that Ching had stuck his hand in the flour barrel and a scorpion had tagged him. He had gone into town for some snakebite remedy—a pint of whiskey.

We always sang to the cattle when we were on night guard. It was necessary. They knew where we were, and we didn't startle them by riding up on them unexpectedly.

I remember one night stampede that almost happened, but I was able to head it off. It was one of those pretty moonlit nights—the sky so clear and the moon so bright that you could have seen to whittle. The cattle were bedded down and quiet. I was riding night guard, just moseying along humming to myself and the cows. Suddenly, I saw a flash up ahead and the cows near it start to milling around and acting nervous. I was on a fast horse, so I took off after that bunch, cut out the leaders, and moved them off to the side to calm down. I walked my horse around the area singing and reassuring those cows until they bedded down again.

As soon as I felt that things were back to normal, I went over to check out the place where I had seen the flash. I saw one of our new hands crawling around in the grass. I stopped and called to him and asked him if he was all right. He answered, "My pony jumped that thar little gully and I lost my wax." I imagine he had been working on that "cud" for days — chewing gum was hard to come by — but he *never* should have jumped off his horse and started lighting matches to look for it. That was what startled those steers and could have started the whole herd running.

Range steers see a man maybe once a year and, in some years, not at all. When they are rounded up, herded together, roped and shoved, they get jittery and nervous. Anything unexpected will set them to running: a clap of thunder, a lurking coyote, a cowhand riding suddenly out of the dark. We rode around them carefully and we sang to them.

If a cowboy couldn't carry a tune, it was sometimes painful to have to listen to him. But he had to make some attempt at a song, and the rest of us just had to suffer along with the cows. I remember one boy who rode around chanting, "Ditty dum, ditty dee," all night long, night after night. Singing calmed the cattle, and it also kept us awake and entertained us throughout the long night and the monotonous ride around the perimeter of the herd.

We sang hymns, old English ballads, nursery rhymes, folk tunes, and made up our own verses. Many a cowboy song was started because a rider got tired of singing the same song over and over so he made up his own and soon the others picked it up. We made up verses about the folks at home, a dream for the future, our girls, and about each other — like the verse about our Bible-reading cook. There was:

*Shootin' and Singin'*

> King's a prince,
> He lives in a tent,
> He wonders where
> His palace went.

And then there were these two I remember:

> Go to sleep little dogie
> Go to sleep old steer
> When you wake up
> I'll still be here.
> When roundup is over
> We'll each go our way.
> You'll go to market
> And I'll get my pay.

Oh, moon, old moon, riding high,
Riding night guard across the sky.
So vast this world that you keep lit
Covering it slowly, bit by bit.
Peeking here — glancing there
Observing all, everywhere;
Watching for strays, bringing them back.
How long's been your duty?
Have you kept track?

13

# Stampedes

There is a song, "Lasca Down by the Rio Grande," that makes me shake my head in disgust every time I hear it, it is so preposterous. The song is about a cowboy trying to stop a night stampede. When he is knocked unconscious his sweetheart throws her body across his and saves his life — or something as ridiculous as that. Anything as silly and unlikely as a cowpuncher having his girl handy while on night guard isn't worth further mention, but I do want to say something on the subject of this tomfool notion of stopping a stampede at night.

When the herd stampeded at night, we just rode out of the way and went back to the wagons, rolled up in our suggans and went to sleep. We knew that there would be plenty of work tomorrow. But ride after them? Or try to get in front of them? Never! Left alone, cattle will usually stop running in a short time and start milling around in small bunches. If some wild-eyed tenderfoot gallops up out of the dark while they are still excited, it will just set them to running again. No, the best thing you can do is turn in and wait until daylight.

One summer we were driving this herd of three thousand steers from our San Angelo range up to better pasture along the Red River. The year 1886 was a bad drought, and our ranges were pretty dry. The Half Circle Six had leased some grazing land to the north and east of Jacksboro where the grass was a little greener.

We were a few miles out of Abilene, moving east, south, and parallel to the Texas and Pacific Railroad right-of-way. The railroad tracks hadn't been there for long and train schedules were irregular. We were not expecting the train that came up behind us, but when we saw it come into view, realizing that those steers had never seen a locomotive before, we knew we were in for trouble.

Tom Rutherford, our trail boss, yelled at us to get between the tracks and the herd. We moved over, leaving the outside flank wide open. When the engineer pulled down on the whistle you can guess what happened! All three thousand of those steers stampeded and they didn't stop until a range of hills, five miles to the south, slowed them down. They ran like Satan was after them, and I am sure that they thought he was.

The stampede started about four in the afternoon, so we made camp right there and gave the cattle the rest of the night to calm down. Then, for the next three days, we rounded up our herd. As I recall, we didn't lose a head.

I believe that bunch of steers was the worst I ever knew for stampeding. They made a run once a night it seemed, and sometimes they put on a matinee. Yep, they held the record in my book.

That same trip, and just a few nights later, we made camp in the Brazos River bottoms. Black clouds moved in and were boiling overhead, lightning flashed in the distance, and the weather was muggy. It was hot; no air was moving. But the cattle were. Instead of bedding down, they kept milling around, getting more and more restless. All hands turned out to ride guard; every one of us was riding around the herd, trying to reassure them and keep them quiet.

This was the night that I first saw the phenomenon called St. Elmo's Fire. The air was charged with electricity. Fireballs formed on the tips of the steers' horns and the whole herd was a sea of small twinkling lights. A crackling, fizzing noise accompanied each flash. Under different circumstances I would have thought it a beautiful sight, but right at that time we had our hands full with our horses, who kept shying, and the frightened steers, who were tossing their heads, wild-eyed with terror.

Then it happened! Lightning struck a tree about a hundred yards away. The resulting thunder sounded like Armageddon was upon us. The sound was deafening, and the herd stampeded in four directions. We backed off and watched as they disappeared into the night; then we met at the wagons and took turns swearing. It took us four days to collect them that time. Some of them were as far away as eight miles.

When we finally wrangled that three thousand head (less the seven we lost during the electrical storm) onto the Red River range, our job was done. Our ranch company had set up a line camp there with cowhands to run it. I was glad to see the last of that crazy herd and relieved to turn around and head for home.

Our group divided; some stayed at the camp, one went to Fort Worth, and six of us headed for the ranch.

14

# Drawing Straws

Our boss, J. H. Ryburn, took the train into Fort Worth to take care of business. He told us to wait for him at the T&P Station at Abilene, and he would ride out to the ranch with us. We rode down on our ponies, leading his horse, and made camp at Buffalo Gap a few miles southwest of Abilene.

One of the boys rode into town and checked at the station to see if Ryburn was waiting for us. He wasn't. Since no westbound train was expected until noon the next day, that night we went into town to enjoy the sights and entertainment.

The next day he didn't come. As it turned out, we waited there four days. Had we checked with general delivery at the post office, we would have gotten his letter telling us that he was delayed in Fort Worth and to stable his horse and proceed to the ranch. Instead, twice a day we met and drew straws. The short straw got to hang around the train station watching for Ryburn while the rest looked for fun, stayed at camp, or hung out at the cattle pens and talked to the local cowboys.

The second day we located a small store, on the edge of town, where there was a side room for thirsty customers. It was a combination grocery, hock shop, and neighborhood bar. The proprietor was a timid, rinsed and wrung-dry sort of little man who seemed overwhelmed by this sudden invasion of five big strangers. I will admit that after three weeks on the trail we looked a little rough and ragged — no fancy-looking sissies, I can tell you.

We spent several hours, the first time we went in, relaxing, drinking beer, killing time, and probably getting louder the longer we drank. Jeff Thomas, as nice a kid as I ever met, started kidding the proprietor, bragging about his reputation as a tough, mean hombre and implying that he was a gunman of renown. We were all laughing at him and backing up his preposterous stories; they were so ridiculous that we never thought anyone would take us seriously. Jeff got up from the table and started toward the bar for another refill. The saloon keeper pulled a gun from under the counter — a "hogleg" with a twelve-inch barrel — and pointed it right at Jeff.

That sobered us all and we froze in surprise. The man said, still pointing his gun at Jeff, "Mister, air ye rilly a badman, or air ye jist a damn fool?"

After we convinced him that we were just joshing him and got him to put away his gun, he told us that he had been held up a few months back and was still edgy and suspicious of strangers. Before we left, he treated us to a round on the house, and we promised to return and patronize his saloon again.

The next morning we took a good look at ourselves and each other and decided that we did look like badmen and needed repairs. We went into town for a bath, shave, and haircut. This splurge pretty well depleted our pocket money. We didn't usually carry money with us on the trail, and we hadn't counted on this four-day stay in Abilene. Anyway, part of our pay was our board, so we did not hesitate to hock Ryburn's horse to the storekeeper for enough to stock up on grub.

Ryburn's train finally pulled in. I had drawn the short straw that morning so I met him and took him by the store, where he paid for our groceries and his horse's stabling. Then we all lit out for the ranch.

As long as Jeff was with the outfit, we kidded him. Someone would yell across the corral or see him in town and call, "Hey, Mister, air ye rilly a badman, or air ye jist a damn fool?"

# 15

# Colorful Language

A bunch of us were in Colorado City, Texas, waiting for a shipment of steers to come by rail from out west. We had been waiting there for several days, meeting trains and killing time between arrivals. One night someone suggested that we go to see Humpty Jones's new honky-tonk. Humpty was a character who floated around West Texas; his principal business was the operation of saloons. He also was a business manager for his "stable."

It was early in the evening when we walked in and things hadn't really gotten started. We got our drinks at the bar and went up to the buzzard roost, where we could have a full view of everything that went on downstairs.

He had one large room with a bar and a dance floor downstairs and the upstairs, which was a balcony overlooking the dance floor. Out back were six shacks, called "cribs," where his girls took their customers. As soon as we sat down and lined up along the balcony railing, the girls started calling up to us and inviting us to come down and dance. There were invitations for other activities, but we just sat there and joked with them and watched the crowd gather.

There were two men in the middle of the dance floor: one was an old man and the other a Mexican. They had tanked up early and were pretty drunk. After awhile they started swearing at each other. They got louder and louder and soon the whole place was listening, laughing at them and egging them on. The cussing and name-calling was getting more and more colorful and being directed at the other customers as well as at each other. When the language got really colorful, old Humpty got between them and shouted loud enough to be heard over the arguing and the audience participation, "Gentlemen, Gentlemen, please watch your language!" Then, pointing to the chippies sitting along the wall, "Can't you see there are ladies present?"

We nearly fell out of the buzzard roost laughing.

We got another lesson in the art of cussing one afternoon when we were working in Runnels County.

We were moving a herd of steers across the Colorado River where there was a shallow ford. The river there was about belly deep to a horse and in the center a little deeper since there had been some rains recently. We had already started the herd across when a buggy carrying two women appeared on the opposite bank. We tried to stop them from driving into the cattle, but they took our waving and shouting as an invitation to proceed, and proceed they did. They met that wall of swimming cattle right in midstream.

The steers began milling around the buggy and, as more cattle entered the river, the congestion and the confusion got worse. One steer caught his horns in the reins and began to pull the buggy and its passengers in a circle; all the time, those women were standing up in the buggy, lashing out at the cows with their buggy whip, holding onto their feathered hats, and shrieking and swearing in a most *unladylike* manner. I hadn't heard such language matched anywhere!

We all plunged in to try to untangle the jam, but we couldn't get to them. Finally, one cowhand stood up on his saddle, jumped over a steer into the buggy, and threw the reins loose so the steer could get untangled. Then the poor horse swam out with the flow of the herd, pulling the buggy back to the bank where it had started.

Our callers were two prostitutes from the red-light district in Ballinger who had heard that we were making camp on the Colorado River that night and had driven out to "give us the keys to the city."

I didn't investigate their other talents but I know this: they were first-rate, top-of-the-line champion cussers.

# 16

# The Nester

Late in 1882, we were down in the Val Verde country on fall roundup. We had taken along a full complement of wranglers, cook, and blacksmith. We camped on Devil's River where there was a good spot for our chuck-wagon and open space to hold a large herd with plenty of water nearby. We were there over two months.

It wasn't unusual to range over a hundred miles looking for strays. Frank King and I drew one of the longer trips over toward the Pecos Valley. We took a pack horse and supplies to last us a week or two.

We picked our way through scrub and cactus, zigzagging across the semi-desert land, checking water holes, making notes as to where the strays were feeding, and mapping out a return route in order to pick them up.

It was in the afternoon of the second day King mentioned that when he had been in this area the year before, he had come upon a "nester" taking up land down in the valley. "Let's angle to the south and see if he is still in this godforsaken place. If he is, why don't we stop by for a spell? I'll allow he don't see many folks."

A respite from the blistering heat that rose from the baked land and the heated rocks and a rest from the long ride sounded good to me. We turned our horses south and headed for the valley, which we could see in the distance.

It was a pretty little valley. We paused and looked down on it from a cliff and could see a creek with willows and cottonwoods making patches of shade on the running stream. Sheep were grazing on the rocky slope near us and we could see more sheep down in the valley floor. The only blot on this pretty scene was a large pile of brown, dead brush under some cottonwood trees.

I had often heard the term *nester,* but this was the first time I had realized the reason why some settlers were given that name. Down below was something that looked like a big, oversized nest; it was a shack surrounded and covered over with cut brush and tree branches woven together to protect the shack and its occupants from predators and the elements. Around it was the biggest mess you ever saw.

As we rode nearer, several dogs rushed out from under the brushpile barking and growling to wake the dead. We were having trouble calming our horses and didn't notice the man with them until we heard him shouting to the dogs, "Aufhort! Kommt!"

He was the picturebook version of a hermit: unkempt beard, long, matted hair, greasy hat, and dirty, torn overalls. He was standing there smiling at us, knee deep in smelly sheep and growling dogs.

His hearty, friendly "Welcome, welcome!" was as cordial as any Rotary Club president's speech to a visiting dignitary. He held his dogs in check while we tied our horses near the creek so they could drink and stand in the shade. He offered us water from his rain barrel, shooed some chickens from a wagon seat he had under the trees, and we sat down to visit.

"I get so lonesome sometimes that I talk to the grass. I don't see folks very often," he said. He spoke with a heavy accent but in very good English. It was obvious that he was a man of some education. He said he was born in Germany and had been in this country about three years. His manner and his appearance were certainly at odds. His name was Schultz.

He invited us into his shack. It was a lean-to with a brush bed on a dirt floor, a table, and two chairs that he had made.

He told us that he was "tidying up for the Missus." When we asked where she was, he explained that he wasn't married yet but expected to marry within the week. In fact, he was leaving the next day for San Antonio to meet his mail-order bride. She was coming by train from the East. He had advertised in a newspaper and made his choice from several who had answered. His bride-to-be was from a large family, had some schooling, and had said that she was used to hard work. He proudly showed us a picture she had sent. She appeared younger than he, and nice looking. I wondered how recent a picture he had sent her and if he had told her about this sheep-smelling hovel and its isolated location. But he was excited and happy with the prospect of companionship, and so we congratulated him and wished him well.

He gave us directions to a watering hole about five miles down the valley where he had seen some cattle. We said good-bye and promised to return and meet his "Missus."

It was about ten days before we came back through, driving a small herd ahead of us. He must have heard us coming, or maybe his dogs alerted him, for he was waiting for us some distance from his shack and hailed us as soon as we rode into view. His appearance was much improved. He had a haircut and was clean-shaven. I realized that he was a much younger man than I had thought and quite nice looking.

He told us, before we inquired, that his bride-to-be had not come but had sent a letter explaining that her father was ill and she was nursing him. She had written that she would be delayed a month and gave him a new arrival time. Later, when the subject came up again, he mentioned that he had sent her money for her passage—one hundred and sixty dollars. King blurted out, "Man, you have been swindled! You will never see her or your money again. She won't come."

I was shocked and embarrassed by King's blunt remark and tried to cover up by making it seem that he was kidding, but Schultz did not take to joking about this and said defensively, "She said that she would come and she will come. You come back next year on your roundup and you will see. She will come!" But he didn't seem to be as confident as he wanted us to think he was. He was disappointed and worried.

We changed the subject by telling him about the country we had been riding through, and soon he was in a better mood. He took us to see a patch of cactus he had ringed with stones to make a garden and described the seeds he had purchased in San Antonio so that they could have flowers the next spring. We stayed longer than we intended for he seemed lonesome, but when he invited us to spend the night, we said that we had to check on our cattle and left. I preferred to bed down away from that overpowering smell of sheep.

The next year, King and I were again sent on the roundup in Val Verde country. We asked for the Pecos Valley assignment. We had often talked about Schultz and how he had been taken for a sucker by that woman in the East. We wanted to check on him and cheer him up with a visit.

We did not stop by his place until the return trip, when we approached through the valley, along the creek. At first we thought that we had taken a wrong turn; we did not recognize his place. The nest of brush was gone and a neat adobe cabin stood under the cottonwoods. A pole fence had been built around a cleared and swept yard so that no sheep could come up around the hose. Schultz's rock-rimmed flower bed was well cared for and showed the remains of summer flowers.

A young woman came out of the house and clapped her hands to call back the dogs that were barking and darting at our horses. She was a good-looker, neat and clean—the word *nice* came to mind.

We took off our hats and introduced ourselves. She said, "I am Mrs. Schultz. My husband has been expecting you. He is out working the sheep but if you will get down and wait, I will ring the bell for him." She brought us a bucket of water and a dipper, then pulled on a rope that hung in a tree. A bell tolled and the sounds echoed against the shoulders of the valley. We complimented her on her fine bell and she said, "It was a wedding present from my husband. I can call him any time I need him. This bell can be heard for miles."

Schultz came in and he, too, had been remodeled. He wore clean, patched overalls and a short, trimmed beard. It was obvious, observing this couple, that they were happy, contented, and very much in love. It was obvious, too, that they would be parents before the new year.

We were invited to stay for dinner, which she set at a table under the cottonwoods. We stayed long enough to inspect their improvements, and Schultz proudly showed us the cradle he was building of bent willow branches. We rode off in early afternoon. As soon as we were out of sight, I turned to King and he to me and we started grinning. He let out a whoop that rivaled the Schultzes' bell.

That was the last year I was sent to that area on roundup, but I heard from the Schultzes through some of the other boys. I would always ask the boys to look in on them when they were in the area. Sometimes I sent gifts and supplies to them. After several years they moved into town so their children could attend school, and I didn't hear of them again except that Schultz was working in a bank.

Many years later, some thirty years or more, I went on a fishing trip down on the Devil's River. I was driving through a little town and remembered it was to this town that Schultz had moved with his young wife and growing family. I stopped, went into the local bank, and inquired if they knew of a Schultz, who had once worked in the bank. The teller came out of his cage and asked me to follow him across the lobby to a door marked "Private." He knocked and opened the door and there sat Schultz — president of the bank.

He was glad to see me and we had a nice visit. He proudly showed me pictures of his family. His children were grown, several of them had college educations, and one was a successful lawyer in the town. This was the son he had made the willow cradle for. On my way out of town I drove past his home, a large Victorian house on a nice, shaded street. There was a woman in the yard with some young children. I recognized Mrs. Schultz and surmised that the children were some of their grandchildren.

That "nester" and his mail-order bride had come a long way.

17

# All Alone

Another year, there was a spring roundup in the Pecos area, west of our range. On the plains the grass is scarce, and because the grazing is poor the cattle wander farther and farther west and have to be rounded up and driven back to better pasture. This type of roundup was usually a cooperative venture between the cattle companies, each ranch would send one or two men to participate. This time the hands were to meet at a windmill in Upton County. We would decide then where to set up our camp and divide up the territory for the cattle search. I was one of the two sent from our outfit.

When the time came to leave our headquarters, my buddy, who was to ride with me, couldn't leave that day and I was instructed to go ahead and meet the rest of the group at the windmill. It is always a mistake to travel alone through uninhabited, unmarked country, but neither I nor anyone else thought that a one-day ride would be a problem. I would probably come upon others from other ranches heading for our rendezvous.

I arrived at the windmill first. No one was there, nor had I seen anyone on the ride over. There was a shack beside the windmill and inside was a bunk and stove. There was a corral for my pony. It was dusk when I arrived so I fixed the salt pork and beans I had brought along and turned in. I wasn't worried; figured that they would pull in the next day.

All the next day I waited and still they did not show up. That night I began to get lonesome, and Upton County is a prime place for lonesomeness. I climbed up on the windmill and looked around me. I could see around, three hundred sixty degrees, for miles and miles, and could not see a man, anything built by man, or any evidence that man had ever been there. It was as if I, that windmill, and the shack were all there was left on this earth. I was feeling light-headed and strange, and hallucinations played tricks on my mind. Wild nightmares picked up those thoughts after I went to sleep.

The third day I woke up sick. I think I got ptomaine poisoning from the food I found in the cabin. I hadn't wanted to eat it but I had eaten all my provisions the first night. All that day I lay there on the cabin floor and rolled and groaned or hung my head out the cabin door. Man, was I sick. I thought I would die, and there were times when I wouldn't have minded if I had.

The fourth day I was too weak to get off the bunk, even to get a drink at the windmill. I slept most of the day. Once I woke, and a Mexican was standing over me. He was dirty and lousy but I was glad to see him. When I woke again, he was giving me a drink of water and there was some soup on the stove that he had made from some dried meat that he had brought with him. By evening I was feeling better. He spoke no English and I no Spanish, but somehow we understood each other. He got out a Mexican deck and we played some monte by lantern light. The little money I had on me I was glad to let him win. He'd had plenty of opportunity to take it from me but he hadn't.

The next day my guardian angel rode off on his burro. I never learned where he had come from nor where he went — not even his name. Maybe he was just that — my guardian angel.

I slept most of the day and woke up about dusk. I pulled

myself up to the platform of the windmill to see if I could see any sign of my party. I was propped up there and got to watching a coyote chasing a jackrabbit. At first, the coyote and the rabbit seemed evenly matched, but when the coyote tired I saw another coyote take up the chase. The cunning of those two coyotes was something of a marvel: one would chase that poor rabbit until he tired, and then he would run the rabbit past the other coyote, who would pick up the pace and chase while his conspirator rested. It took a long time to wear down that rabbit. As soon as he showed signs of weakening both coyotes took up the chase. Even though they were working together, it was evident that neither trusted the other. Finally, they put on a great burst of speed. Running shoulder-to-shoulder, they overtook their prey, scooped him up, threw him high, and caught him midair on the way down. They tugged and fought over that jackrabbit until they each had a part. One of the coyotes got the short ration, but he just had to make do.

I was saddling my horse the next morning, preparing to return to the ranch when a rider came up. He said the rest of the group was behind him and would be along in a few hours. They had run into a bunch of ranging cattle they hadn't expected to find and had lost several days hazing the herd back toward the northeast. They hadn't known I was waiting at the windmill. They had been told we were held up at the Half Circle Six Ranch and would be late arriving. My buddy had come up on them that morning, and it was then they realized that I had been waiting for them for six days.

It was the last time I ever went on an assignment alone. And I have been overly picky about my food ever since.

# 18

# Revivals

A cowpuncher leads a rather solitary life. Sure, there were other cowhands around, but much of our time was spent alone — riding alone at night, off somewhere repairing fences or windmills, spending weeks at a line camp on roundup, or just being at the ranch, which was far from its nearest neighbor.

The life of a cowboy was a life among men; there were very few females around a ranch and none in the camps — at least, that was my experience. Single women were scarce in West Texas, and any woman not ugly enough to scare a dog off a gut wagon married at an early age. There was little enough romance, I can tell you, and any chance we got to meet young women, at church, at a social in town, or at a rare dance at the ranch, was a big event for the year.

We would ride miles to attend any event where we could be with young people our age. If we heard there was to be a dance in one of the towns around, as tired as we were after weeks of manhandling those steers, we would come in, clean up, and get to that dance, somehow. And they were glad to have us attend; without the boys from the ranches they wouldn't have had much of a crowd, or much music either. Some of our boys were fair fiddlers, and Will Pine was the best banjo picker I ever knew. If enough of our boys knew girls whom they could invite, we sometimes threw a dance at our ranch headquarters. Each girl would bring her whole family and it would turn out to be a large affair. We would get everything cleaned up and looking nice and even fix supper and refreshments for our guests. We didn't do this often, but when we did, it was a first-rate party.

We went to an occasional box supper at a schoolhouse and, now and then, to a church social. I always enjoyed the spelling bees that were held as part of the entertainment, and I usually won. If I did miss a word, I would raise my eyes and say thanks that Grandpa hadn't been there to witness my disgrace. He would have tanned my hide, for sure.

We attended revivals—brush arbor meetings, we called them. The brush arbors were all built alike. Nearly every town had one. They would get to looking rather shabby between meetings, but when the local citizens knew that a preacher was coming to hold a revival, everyone turned out and repaired the brush arbor.

The site of the arbor was usually where there was a stand of trees. A few trees were chopped down, the larger trunks put up for a sapling frame. The branches and small limbs were thrown on top of the frame for shade or protection when a shower would blow in—a rare event in West Texas.

There was never enough room under the arbor for all the people who came—and they came from miles around, especially for a Holy Roller meeting or to hear a good Baptist "fire-breather." There were always people sitting outside under the trees or in their wagons and buggies, especially young couples. Occasionally you would hear some father walking between the wagons calling, "Lizzie, you out here? Lizzie, you come sit under the arbor with your ma and me." But you never heard Lizzie answer back.

The preachers were always good. They gave us something to ponder on all the next week: how we were on the sure path to hell and there wasn't much hope for us since we hadn't gone down front when he had given us the opportunity to have hands laid on us. The women were there with their palmleaf fans, and the men sweated under their unaccustomed coats and ties. The babies cried, then went to sleep on their fathers' shoulders. We all fought the blisterbugs and didn't realize until we got home that we had lost the battle.

And the singing! I enjoyed that the most. I tried to arrive early because we would start the singing as soon as the pianist arrived and sing until the preacher thought that everyone had come who was coming. I have helped move many a piano to get the singing started sooner. We would start at the front of the hymnbook and sing all the way through to the psalms in the back, before the revival ended, repeating our favorites every night.

Each family brought a lantern and hung it on the arbor where they could keep an eye on it. We had to be careful of fire. Young boys liked to swing on the frame to show off, and that would set the lanterns to swinging and swaying. I have seen many a spanking administered right there at prayer meeting, with the little girls giggling at the embarrassment of their suitors who had been performing for them. I identified with those young fellows, for I remembered the same humiliation back in Grapevine and the hiding my Uncle Garley had given me for chinning myself at a revival.

I always stayed to watch the breakup of a service at night. As each family left they would take down their lantern and walk off with it. Finally the preacher would blow out the last light. Everything would be dark and quiet. The moon would light up the empty space where, just a short time before, there had been wagons and people laughing and talking. The meeting was over. I always thought of that moment as the benediction.

When we were camping down on Devil's River, our cook told us that there was a brush arbor meeting at a crossroads about seven miles away. We had been looking at the same bunch of wranglers and the same steers for some weeks, so Will Parr, Kirk Page, and I decided we would ride over that night, attend a service, enjoy the singing, and see some new faces.

We could hear the singing some distance away. There were wagons, buckboards, buggies, and saddle horses surrounding the place. We tied our ponies to some bushes and walked toward the arbor just as the singing stopped and the preacher commenced. We found a place to sit on some logs, outside of the lighted area and behind the preacher.

His sermon was short; his text was "Suffer little children to come unto me." After his sermon and the passing of the collection plate, he announced that this night he would baptize the babies who had been born since he had been there the year before. He called for the babies to be brought forward. It seemed that half the congregation came to the front. There were thirty-two babies—we counted them. With the babies were their parents and grandparents. Younger children were running around and whispering to their parents, and older brothers and sisters were tugging at them to make them return to their seats. It was total chaos but the preacher soon had the situation in hand; everyone lined up on a side aisle. He had a system: he would motion for a family to step up to the font, he would ask the name of the baby, scoop a handful of water, and call loudly, "I baptize. . . ." The family would move on and another would come forward. It was the same for all.

Will whispered, "The calf crop has been good this year but last year was better. Most in this bunch look more like yearlings."

We sat through the first dozen baptisms and could see that the ceremony would go on for some time more. We were making our move to leave when we got interested in the names of the babies. The girls had a variety of names—no special trend there—but the boys all seemed to have one of three names: Martin Luther, John Calvin, or John Wesley. When a family would start forward, we would each whisper "boy" or "girl."

We were doing pretty well guessing the sex of the babies because the little girls were dressed in frilly clothes. When we each said "Boy," we would place a nickel on the log and pick a name: Martin Luther, John Calvin, or John Wesley. It was winner take all.

There was one husky, clabber-headed, bald baby who had captured our attention right at the beginning. The mother of this kid was a grim-faced, wiry little woman, and her child was giving her a hard time, twisting and turning, pulling her hair and butting her in the face. Will had already made some comment that in just a year or two we could hire that one to help us with roping and branding. When this baby and family stepped forward we all said "Boy." I put my nickel down and took Martin Luther, Kirk took John Calvin, and that left John Wesley for Will. We leaned forward to hear the preacher ask his question and the mother give the baby's name.

The woman called out proudly, "Mary Ann Lizbeth."

With that, the three of us rolled backwards off the log, grabbed our hats, and crawled off toward our horses, choking and trying to hold back our laughter until we could get out of earshot.

There was a revival in Knickerbocker one summer, and the preacher was a Campbellite. I wasn't in the area while the meeting was being held, but it must have been one of the biggest they ever had—before or since. There were so many converts from this revival that a local congregation of Campbellites was formed. They built a little church and held Wednesday night prayer meetings and Sunday services. Before the revivalist left town, he laid down the guidelines, and they were "straight and narrow." The members set about restructuring their lives and everybody else's. They were out to clean up the town.

Two of the boys from the Half Circle Six were members of this group. They had marched down together at the revival and joined on the first night. Art and John were as loyal and faithful as any member in the church. They attended every service, spent all their spare time helping with the building, and took up a collection at the ranch to help finance it. They were always urging others to go to church with them and often we did. But there was one guideline that they did not follow: they liked their Saturday night entertainment and their liquor. I never saw either of them drunk or disorderly, but when we went into town and went into the local bar, they put their feet on the brass railing and drank with the rest of us.

Their fellow church members took this as a challenge. They harassed them in church, on the street, in town, and even came out to the ranch to read the Bible to them. They never gave up, and Art and John never buckled under. It was a standoff.

A year after the forming of that church, they held another revival, and the preacher who had organized their group returned for their anniversary celebration. The first service was to be on Sunday, and afterward there would be "dinner on the ground." It was to be a big affair and the whole town was invited. After work Saturday night, Art and John went in to help set up extra chairs and tables out under the trees where the dinner would be served. They made arrangements with the ranch cooks to furnish the potato salad and that was their assigned contribution. They were excited and invited us to be their guests. We were up long before daylight on Sunday to do our chores so we could go in for church. We went in and filled up the last pew at the rear of the building.

The minister was in his best form. He shouted, threatened, and he went on and on and on. His subject was "The Evils of Liquor." And when he would point, his finger seemed to reach all the way to the back of the church. If Art and John realized that determined reformer was out to get them, they gave no signs. I felt very uncomfortable and was relieved when the sermon ended with a thundering finale. Then the preacher stood there looking directly at Art and John and said hoarsely,

"While we sing all verses of 'Bringing in the Sheaves' all who swear to forego the drinking of spirits, FOREVER, file by and shake my hand."

Row by row, the members got up and went forward to shake his hand, even the children, the local bartender, and the town drunks. At last our row was the only one left. I wanted to jump through the window, but I just sat there with my buddies while the congregation turned to stare at us. They finished the last verse and started over. Still, Art and John sat there, looking at the ceiling and acting as if nothing was unusual.

After an interminable time, the singing stopped but the silence was deafening. The preacher was as puffed as a toad and he was red in the face, he was so mad. He was screeching when he called for Art and John to come to the front of the church. They marched up, shoulder to shoulder, with heads held high.

"Young fellers," he said, his voice shaking and his eyes glaring something fierce, "You are *sinners!* You inbibe the evilest of drink. You *will not* repent!" He waited several seconds and there wasn't so much as a rustle from the congregation. Then he shouted, "THE CONGREGATION IS WITHDRAWING FROM YOU!" Then we heard John's voice say, "But Deacon, ya'll can't do that. Why, Art and me don't know nothin' about running a church."

They stood there while the preacher gave the benediction and the congregation hurried out. We walked up and led John and Art out to our horses, and we all rode back to the ranch. They were in a daze. We didn't talk about what had happened, nor did the subject ever come up later.

To my way of thinking, that preacher did the Lord no favor and that congregation lost two of their best members.

# 19

# The Big City

I knew many old trail drivers who had been up the trail to Dodge City and Abilene, Kansas, to take cattle to market. The days of trail herding were over by the time I began going with the cattle to market. After the Texas-Pacific Railroad was laid into Colorado City and the Santa Fe Railroad came into Ballinger, Texas, our cattle were moved to market by rail. We shipped from both places, but mostly from Ballinger. We shipped to Chicago.

We looked forward to these trips to Chicago, but I wonder, now, why we did. We slept in a dirty caboose, were up all night making inspection, prodding steers to keep them on their feet, unloading to feed, and reloading. Chicago was cold by anyone's standard and especially by a southerner's. The wind off that lakefront was so cold and wet that it made your head ache just to breathe it. And the confidence men! We finally realized that we just couldn't wear our Texas clothes there—especially our big hats—this just made the slicks close in.

Usually a cowboy had a good hat and a good pair of boots and he didn't give a hoot what went between. But if you went to market in Chicago, you had your work clothes and your city clothes. Most years you didn't get to wear your dress clothes between one market trip and the next. The first year I went, I bought myself a bowler, vest, button shoes, and a cutaway

suit. The most important purchases were my overcoat, muf-
fler, and gloves. Even dressed in these I was colder than I ever
was out riding in our worst Texas blizzard.

After we arrived at the market, we worked hard unloading,
caring for, and feeding our cattle until they were sold. The ranch
owners went with us and usually had several days of business
to take care of after the sale, so we had time to look around,
take the streetcars out from the downtown area, and attend
some of the vaudeville shows. It was a break in the monotony
and a chance to compare city life with our way of living — and
I never knew anyone who said they wanted to trade.

I kept a diary then, as I have ever since, but at that time
it wasn't a day-by-day account as now, but just a record of things
I needed to remember: expenses, cattle brands I observed on
the ranges, people I met, cattle sales.

This record of expenses was kept on one of the Chicago trips:

| Fort Worth | suit of riding clothes | $ 3.50 |
| | waist coat | .60 |
| | shirt | 1.00 |
| | cuff buttons | .40 |
| | pair socks | .25 |
| Kansas City | pair gloves | 1.50 |
| Chicago | overcoat | 14.00 |
| | scarf | .60 |
| Rec'd cash from Ryburn | | |
| | Ballinger | $10.00 |
| | Fort Worth | 5.00 |
| | Kansas City | 7.00 |
| | Chicago | 50.00 |

There is this entry: "December 15, 1887, laying up in Arkansas City today, the longest day in all my travels. I was on my
way to Chicago with cattle and Ryburn and I got left in Fort
Worth. We caught up in Arkansas City."

When we loaded in Ballinger, we always stopped in Fort Worth for our first feed and water stop, and sometimes stayed over a day. This particular trip, Ryburn had some business to take care of and for some reason I was tagging along that day. We got back to the stockyards late and found that the train had pulled out without us. We hung the next freight and set out to catch up with our outfit at the next scheduled watering stop.

As soon as we saw the cattle pens in Arkansas City, Kansas, we swung off and started looking for our boys. We hadn't known there were two areas of cattle pens, and our pens were three miles down the track. Have you ever walked three miles along a railroad track in high-heeled boots? Those boots are fine when you need a heel to dig in when you have a wild cow on one end of a rope and are holding onto the other end and skimming along on the ground, or to keep your foot from slipping through the stirrup when you are hanging onto a bucking horse. But our boots were never meant for walking three miles on crushed rock and railroad ties. We wore the skin off our heels, arches, and all ten toes.

We finally found our outfit and got an awful rawhiding for missing the train—and got precious little sympathy for our bloody feet.

That same trip, a young kid turned up in Kansas City. He was just about the age I was when I left home—not much older, if any. He was a hobo, a drifter. He approached us and asked if he could ride in our caboose—said that he would make a hand helping with the cattle if he could sleep where it was warm. Ryburn even told him that he would pay him a little something, and he joined up with us. He and I shared shifts. His name was Jake. There was something about Jake that reminded me of Arch Davis. Maybe it was just that I was in the role of the teacher and protector as Arch had been. I showed him the ropes and looked out for him.

As we traveled north, the weather got worse. We rode through

as bad a snow and sleet storm as I have ever seen. When the
train would stop, we got out to make inspection. We would
peer into the cars, and if a steer was down, we would prod him
to make him get up—a cow could be trampled to death if he
stayed down. We rarely finished our duty before the train would
start up and then we would hang on, climb up, and walk along
the top of the cars until we reached the caboose and then swing
through the trapdoor. That was one part of the job I never liked
nor got used to. When the weather was as bad as on this particular trip, we found ourselves running on top of a speeding
train with a coat of ice underfoot and a blowing gale blind-
ing us.

The night before we pulled into Chicago, Jake and I drew
a midnight inspection. It was sleeting and the temperature
was below zero. Jake was working the front of the train and
I was about halfway back when the train started up. I grabbed
a ladder rung and climbed to the top of the car, then started
working my way toward the rear of the train. That narrow catwalk was one sheet of ice. I was slipping and sliding and skid-
ding along when the train gave a sudden jerk. I fell backward
and went skating along the walkway on the seat of my pants.
I would have gone down between two cars if I hadn't grabbed
a brake handle at the end of the car and wrapped my leg around
it to straddle it. I just sat there, hugging the brake handle,
and shook more from fright than from the cold; I had lost my
nerve completely. I knew I would freeze to death if I continued to sit there, but I couldn't move.

I couldn't have been anchored to the brake handle for more
than two minutes (it seemed longer) when I heard Jake trot-
ting along the catwalk behind me. As he came upon me, he
gave me a slap on the back and said, "Get up, you big baby!"
Then he jumped to the next car and stood there laughing at
me. It made me mad enough that my blood started warming.
I got up and took off after him.

Jake disappeared as soon as we pulled into Chicago. He didn't even say good-bye. He was a good hand. We would have taken him back to the ranch with us and made a wrangler of him.

I have thought of him often and can see him now on the top of that train, his hands in his pocket, whistling and strolling along like he was walking down a country lane. And I wonder, if he hadn't come into my life when he did and found me that night in the blizzard, would I ever have let go of that brake handle?

# 20

# A Little Dogie

I was as satisfied with my job and as happy working on the Half Circle Six Ranch as I felt I could be anywhere, but when I turned twenty-seven, I began to feel a need to plan something more permanent for my future. I think that the incident on the train had something to do with my change in attitude. I know that my brother Albert's death definitely did.

Looking around me, I began to notice men grown too old or disabled to handle ranch jobs, but still hanging around the fringes of the cattle business, taking any odd job they could find. I didn't want to grow old working for the other man, and I wasn't sure that I wanted to grow old wrangling cattle. I wanted a home and a family and a lady for a wife — the kind of woman I just couldn't picture living in some of the run-down cabins that dotted the landscape around West Texas. I had never known a home of my own, never felt a part of a community. I wanted roots, to be a part of the life of a town, a member of a church, active in the politics of my state.

When Mama and I used to talk together, she would reminisce about the happiest segment of her life, before the war, when she was a bride and a young wife and mother, and her husband owned the general store in New Danville. She had described the life of a merchant as a clean, satisfying occupation, where the father and husband came home for dinner and slept every night in his own bed. I sometimes imagined, and there is a lot of time to do that on night guard, that I lived in a pretty little town where I owned a pretty little house and had a pretty little wife and a store where I presided as proud owner. Once, when driving a herd into Fort Worth, I passed through a corner of Palo Pinto County where the creek ran clear and the pastures looked green and the town of Strawn looked like that town in my dreams. I had planned ever since to go back to that place and see if it really was the place I remembered.

In the summer of 1888 fate stepped in and this bit of fate stepped in on four legs, right in the path of my horse. That morning I was cutting out cows and was riding one of the best cuttin' horses I ever owned; just show that pony the cow you wanted and you didn't have to touch a rein. He was right in after a steer and hazing him down an open space, going full tilt, when a little dogie ran out and dodged right into our path. The horse and calf tangled and we went down; my head hit a rock and I was out cold. The horse was up almost before his knees hit the ground and started running, dragging me with my foot caught in the stirrup. One of the boys took off after us, roped my horse, and stopped him. They stretched me out under a tree.

They said that I was unconscious for a couple of hours and was dazed for several weeks afterward. They told me later that I walked around with a silly grin on my face and hummed snatches of songs. I remember very little of that time, just that my head hurt. Ryburn wouldn't let me work, and I stayed around headquarters.

One night I was restless and couldn't get to sleep. Sometime after midnight I walked out of the bunkhouse and sat under the tree in the moonlight. One second I was sitting there in a kind of stupor, my head hurting like it had never hurt before, and the next second the hurting stopped and all was clear. It was as if a thick gray fog just rolled away, like coming to the surface after swimming under water. I have been told since that at that second a blood clot in my brain dissolved.

I was too excited then to sleep, and I sat there for the rest of the night looking at the ranch in that clear bright moonlight. I thought about some of the cowboys I had known who had accidents and were punch drunk and disabled for the rest of their lives. I knew it had come very close to happening to me. I thought about Mama and Dick and, for the first time in ten years, I was homesick. It was as clear to me as that moonlight that I had been given a sign. If I was to live out my life as I wanted to and had dreamed it to be, I had better get started.

When the sun came up, I looked around the ranch and knew that I was saying good-bye to a way of life and a part of my state that I loved. But I had things to do and places to go. I had a Lady to meet.

It was time to move on.

# Epilogue

*March 12, 1930*

> *I slept round the clock, last night, from 7 to 7;*
> *had the most beautiful dream. I was a boy again,*
> *saw all the horses on the old ̄6 Ranch . . . saw the 14*
> *head I used to ride. All the horses were fat and there*
> *was pretty green grass everywhere with wet-weather*
> *springs running. But when I woke it made me feel*
> *sad to realize that I was not young again, but was*
> *climbing up into old age.*

—from the diary of Malcolm Graham Vernon,
at age sixty-nine

Malcolm Vernon moved to Palo Pinto County, Texas, in 1891 and opened a general store. His stationery was headed:

office of
M. G. VERNON
Staple and Fancy Groceries
Confectionaries, Notions, etc.
Strawn, Texas

He built a house on the east boundary of the town and beyond that had a pasture for a few head of cattle. It was to this home that he brought his bride. Here they raised their children (who all married in the parlor), and three of their grand-children were born here. They both died in this home, Emma in 1935 and Malcolm in 1936. They are buried in the Strawn Cemetery, as are their children and grandchildren.

Nancy Emma Lewis was born in Forney, Texas, on May 3, 1870. She was the second child and eldest daughter of Leona Dunnica and John Madison Lewis. She was educated in the Forney Public School, Lewis Academy, Ursuline Academy in Dallas, and received her B.A. degree, with honors, from the Sherman Female Institute, Mary Nash College, in 1891. She and Malcolm met when she visited friends in Strawn, Texas.

"I saw her when she arrived on the noon train and I knew then that this was my Lady. I rushed over to assist her with her luggage and was introduced to her by her hostess." This Malcolm told to his grandchildren, many years later. "That afternoon I sent a note to her asking if I might escort her to a party being given in her honor that evening — after first getting permission from her host, a Mr. Rhea of our city. She visited in Strawn for a week, we corresponded that winter, and the next spring I went to Forney to meet her family and ask for her hand in marriage. We married in the Methodist Church of Forney on June 23, 1892. We were married 43 happy years."

Malcolm Vernon, called "Mac" by his friends, "Papa" by his children and grandchildren, and "Mr. Vernon" by his wife, served on the school board and was mayor of his town. He was active in the politics of his city, county, and state. In 1901 he sold his store and opened an insurance agency, which he operated until his death.

This tribute to him, by one of his many, many friends, was published in the newspaper after his death:

> When I became acquainted with Mr. Vernon I was attracted to his seemingly inexhaustible fund of common sense and apparent dislike of anything that savored of sham and hypocrisy. This rare logic of his ripened into a philosophy — and to me

he was ever a philosopher with a sense of humor. I, like many others, went to him for counsel and guidance and if he ever gave anything but the soundest advice I failed to discover it. To me, a tenderfoot from the deep South, Mr. Vernon was the symbol of the West. He loved his state because he knew it so well and he was as naturally a part of it as its hills, valleys and plains. And yet, he was not provincial in his thinking. His love of reading made him a citizen of the world with an uncanny knowledge of world affairs. His keen satire, tinged with a natural wit, made him seem to me an Elbert Hubbard and a Mark Twain in composite.*

And this from his obituary:

Mr. Vernon held a high place in the growth of Strawn and Palo Pinto County where his cheerful and amiable disposition won hundreds of lasting friendships for him. He was always a friend of education, law and order, and ever ready to extend charity to the needy. He was loved by the entire citizenship.

Mr. Vernon was known as an influence in the political fortunes of his city, county and state; his advice was sought and listened to by many.

Texas has lost another of her few remaining pioneer cowboys, a true patriot and a valued citizen.†

*_Strawn Tribune_, Feb. 13, 1936.
†*Strawn Tribune*, Feb. 6, 1936.

*Under the Texas Sun* was composed into type on a Compugraphic digital phototypesetter in eleven point Garamond with two points of spacing between the lines. Garamond was also selected for display. The book was designed by Jim Billingsley, typeset by Metricomp, Inc., printed offset by Thomson-Shore, Inc., and bound by John H. Dekker & Sons. The paper on which the book is printed bears acid-free characteristics for an effective life of at least three hundred years.

*Texas A&M University Press  :  College Station*